Steps to the Top

ALSO BY ZIG ZIGLAR

See You at the Top (1974)
Confessions of a Happy Christian (1978)
Dear Family (1984)

Zig Ziglar

Steps to the Top

PELICAN PUBLISHING COMPANY

GRETNA 1988

First printing, May 1985
Second printing, September 1985
Third printing, April 1986
Fourth printing, December 1987

Library of Congress Cataloging in Publication Data

Ziglar, Zig.
   Steps to the top.

   1. Success. 2. Conduct of life. I. Title.
BJ1611.2.Z54   1985   158'.1   85-3428
ISBN 0-88289-460-9

Manufactured in the United States of America
Published by Pelican Publishing Company, Inc.
1101 Monroe Street, Gretna, Louisiana 70053

Contents

Preface

I seriously question whether there is a person anywhere who does not, from time to time, have some "down" moments. In my judgment, the best way to avoid those is to work at being "up." *Steps to the Top* was written with the hope, belief, and conviction that if you will spend just a few minutes each day with positive thoughts, you will have the lift that you need to succeed. You can pick up the book and read one page for a temporary lift, you can read several success steps and become more solidly founded with uplifting material, or you can involve yourself in the Action Steps and receive more long-lasting benefits.

The way to benefit the most is to share these hints with other members of the family and those with whom you work. The old adage that the teacher learns more than the pupil is more than just a thought. Those who give truly benefit more than those who receive. *Steps to the Top* was written not only to give you a lift, but to help you become a giver. I encourage—and challenge—you to share this information.

Really dig into these steps to success. Pick this book up at a moment's notice, read several pages the first thing in the morning, and read some the last thing at night. When you've completed the book, start over and receive even greater benefits.

I don't know your particular situation, but chances are excellent that in these pages you will find people who were infinitely worse off than you, who triumphed over their difficulties because of their thoughts, beliefs, and actions. Many of those same thoughts, beliefs, and actions will benefit you enormously. I encourage you, therefore, to get busy, get involved, get going in *Steps to the Top*, and I'll "see *you* at the top!"

Thank You

*I*t's difficult to say thank you to the world—or even to America—but in many ways *Steps to the Top* represents my attempt to do exactly that. Thank you, America, for giving me the opportunity, through freedom and the free enterprise system, to write this book. Thank you to the men and women, boys and girls, whose stories grace these pages and have inspired me as well as the countless thousands who have heard them on my radio program.

There are five particular people, though, who certainly deserve double super-special thank-yous. I start with Jim Savage, who is the vice president of the corporate training division of the Zig Ziglar Corporation. Jim did a magnificent job of working with me in assembling the material, sorting it out, and correcting the grammatical errors that crept in despite my best efforts. Jim's specific suggestions on some of the Action Steps were invaluable; much of the book's value can be laid at his doorstep.

Thank you to Stephen Douglas Williford, Grady James Robinson, and Dr. Neil Gallagher for contributing some of the stories in *Steps to the Top*. Your research efforts were essential; your assistance was badly needed, most appreciated, and will be most beneficial to the readers.

Finally, thank you Laurie Downing for your untiring efforts in typing the manuscript. I know that by now you are accustomed to doing this work, nevertheless, your skill never ceases to amaze me. Your speed on our word processor, your accuracy in what you do, and most of all your spirit of helpfulness have truly been significant in the writing and publication of this book.

To the other members of my staff who have made contributions I again say thank you. My thanks and gratitude, also, to the members of my family, especially the Redhead, who has been my wife and my life for over thirty-seven years. Her constant love and inspiration is a prime reason *Steps to the Top* and all my other efforts reach fruition.

Steps to the Top

Attitude . . .

The important and decisive factor in life is not what happens to us, but the attitude we take toward what happens.

. . . and Inferiority

*T*here are moments in all our lives when we feel below par and have brief moments of doubt. As a matter of fact, the late Dr. Maxwell Maltz has written, "At least ninety-five percent of the people in the world feel inferior." The reason so many people feel inferior about their own lives, looks, skills, and abilities is because we spend too much time comparing ourselves with heroes and heroines from the make-believe world of television.

Every teenage girl feels she must rate at least a "10" or she will not be acceptable to her classmates.

Every teenage boy feels that he must be a combination of Tom Selleck and Joe Theismann rolled into one.

Every father feels that he must be a super success in business before he is acceptable as a father.

Our problem is that we make the mistake of comparing ourselves with other people. You are you and you don't have to measure up to any other person. You are not inferior or superior to any human being. The creator has created each and every one of us with a touch of uniqueness and originality. You do not determine your success by comparing yourself to others, rather you determine your success by comparing your accomplishments to your capabilities. You are "number one" when you do the best you can with what you have every day.

Action Steps

1. Today I will realize that I am special and unique, and I will use my talents instead of wishing for the talents of another.
2. Today I will_____

_____

Why is it we judge ourselves by our ideals and others by their acts?

. . . and Blessings

*T*his is a very good time to be living, because the "good ole days" may not have been so good after all.

Every generation has experienced its share of problems. Some people today emphasize the negative and forget the positive. One hundred years ago life expectancy was less than forty years; today we are expected to live to be over seventy-four.

Just a few years ago, polio was the fear of every mother when she sent her son or daughter outside to play during the hot summer months. Last year there were only eighty-six cases of polio reported in this country.

One hundred years ago men wore six-shooters, sanitation was primitive, childbirth was hazardous, and the bathroom was behind the house. Today we have more young people in college than ever before. We have more minority youth in college becoming doctors, lawyers, teachers, and ministers than ever.

As a matter of fact, I'm absolutely convinced that one day we will look back and say that the 1980s were the greatest ten years of this century. We are living in a great era. It's a good time to be living, working, and raising a family. *These* are the "good ole days."

Action Steps

1. Today I will count my blessings; five things I am especially grateful for are: a) _____ b) _____ c) _____ d) _____ e) _____ .
2. Today I will_____

_____

Happiness is not a station at which you arrive, but a manner of traveling.

. . . and Criticism

Davy Crockett had a simple motto: "Make sure you are right, then go ahead." Every one of us, like every successful person you will ever meet, faces moments of criticism. No matter what your career involvement, the more successful you become, the more criticism you will receive. Only those who don't attempt anything remain forever above criticism.

Being criticized is not a problem if you develop a positive way of dealing with it. Winston Churchill had framed on the wall of his office the following words of Abe Lincoln: "I do the very best I can, I mean to keep going. If the end brings me out all right, then what is said against me won't matter. If I'm wrong, ten angels swearing I was right won't make a difference." Churchill received much criticism in his lifetime and Abe Lincoln was roundly criticized in his day, just as most of our public figures are today. It takes a person of great courage to forge ahead and do what he honestly believes to be right when critics are howling against him.

Remember that all the water in the world won't sink your boat if it doesn't get inside. Rise above it. Make certain you are right, and then stand by your convictions. If you do, I'll see you at the top!

Action Steps

1. Today I will repeat the words of Abe Lincoln when criticism comes my way, and I will rise above the critics.
2. Today I will _____

_____

Don't be afraid of opposition. Remember, a kite rises against—not with—the wind.

Hamilton Mabie

15

. . . and Variety

*Y*ou've heard it said that we should never change a proven success formula. Generally speaking, I agree with that statement. But sometimes there is a time and place for a change of recipe in almost any area of business. For example, potato chips are an American tradition, a very successful sales item. That fact didn't keep Procter and Gamble a few years ago from launching "Pringles," a product that defied tradition and opened up a whole new market.

On occasion the ingredient for success is the surprise element. For example, Coach Tom Landry of the Dallas Cowboys is well-known for having a surprise for his opponent in an especially big game. He is well aware that the opponent will be prepared for the standard stuff, so he often catches them off guard with his innovations.

What about you? Think it through carefully, then if the situation warrants, change the recipe. Add the special ingredients of optimism, enthusiasm, courtesy, and positive thinking. Your innovation could be the surprise that will catch your competition off guard—and give you the winning edge!

Action Steps

1. Today I will watch for the opportunity to be innovative, and if the situation warrants, I will change the recipe.
2. Today I will_____

_____

If you want to succeed you should strike out on new paths rather than travel the worn paths of accepted success.

John D. Rockefeller, Sr.

. . . and Humor

*W*ith the right attitude and a touch of humor you can do what Mal Hancock did. Mal took the proverbial lemon of a paralyzing fall and turned that tragedy into real-life lemonade. Mal was in high school, facing a promising career in athletics, when a fall paralyzed him from the waist down. He endured some heartbreaking days trying to make the mental and physical adjustments.

There are no guarantees, as Mal Hancock learned, that life will be a bed of roses. On the contrary, you can count on facing some very strange events, but if you learn to face the unexpected with humor and optimism, you too can come out on top. While in the hospital Mal began to draw the scenes around him. Rather than complain about the nurse waking him at 3 A.M. for a sleeping pill, he drew a cartoon about it that made the point with a laugh. Soon all the nurses in the hospital were coming by to see what Mal had chosen to draw.

It wasn't long before he had sold one of those cartoons to a magazine. That single sale launched him into a successful career as a cartoonist. Today Mal Hancock's name can be read on cartoons in the *Saturday Evening Post* and *T.V. Guide*. Incidentally, his first book was called—you guessed it—*Hospital Humor*.

Mal learned a lesson which can be important to all of us. Even when you can't do anything about a situation (such as being paralyzed), you can do a lot about your *attitude* toward the situation.

Action Steps

1. Today I will laugh *with* others as often as possible, remembering to take my family and my business seriously, but not to take myself too seriously.
2. Today I will _____
   _____

Perhaps man, having remade his environment, will turn around at last and begin to remake himself?

Will Durant

. . . and Belief

*I*ntense belief in a goal is one of the most powerful forces on earth. Joan of Arc was a twelve-year-old shepherd girl when she developed the belief that she would lead the army of France against England. The intensity of her belief was overwhelming. At age seventeen she appeared before and explained her belief to Prince Charles, who was so impressed he gave her a suit of armor and an army to lead. Joan of Arc then led a successful siege against the supposedly unconquerable bastion of Orleans.

To repeat myself, intense belief in a cause or goal is one of the most *powerful* forces on earth. No matter what the odds may be, or how insurmountable the barriers appear, belief dictates that there is a way. The armor for your belief and goals may take the form of a stethoscope, a typewriter, or a microphone. Your sword may be patience, unselfishness, or a never-say-die attitude.

I believe success is achieved by ordinary people with *extra*ordinary determination. Notice that I didn't say it would be easy. Worthwhile accomplishments seldom are.

Action Steps

1. Today I will intensify the most powerful force on earth—my belief—by closely examining what I believe to be important in the physical, mental, and spiritual areas of my life.
2. Today I will _____

_____

He does not believe that does not live according to his belief.

Thomas Fuller

. . . and Talent

*T*ilda Kemplen grew up and still lives in the rugged mountains of East Tennessee. She went to a one-room school through the eighth grade, and then *repeated* the eighth grade because there was no high school to attend. Later, as a cook for a Methodist Mission school, she became determined to go back to school. She enrolled in high school at age 32—with a husband, three small children, a job as a cook, and a home to keep—and graduated five years later. Then she earned a college degree in early education.

Tilda wanted to help the mountain children avoid the problems she experienced. She wanted to establish a program for them, but there were no funds and no buildings. So Tilda volunteered her time and held class in the fields. Later, she raised funds for a child development center, which has employed over six hundred persons in a county with a twenty-six-percent unemployment rate. Tilda, who recently in Washington received the Jefferson Award for outstanding public service, says, "Everybody has some talent. If I can do it, you can too."

Think about it. It's not your situation, but what you make of that situation, which determines what you will accomplish with your life.

Action Steps

1. Today I will spend more time thinking about what I do have rather than what I don't have.
2. Today I will_____

_____

Our business in life is not to get ahead of others, but to get ahead of ourselves.
Stewart B. Johnson

. . . and Dishonesty

A branch of the Justice Department recently released the results of a three-year survey on dishonesty in the workplace. James K. Stewart, director of the National Institute of Justice, said the report indicates that employee theft is costing American business five to ten *billion* dollars a *year!*

Of even greater significance is the "time stealing" that takes place. The average white-collar worker steals four hours and eighteen minutes each week by arriving late, leaving early, taking excessively long coffee and lunch breaks, smoking, making personal phone calls, and so forth. Many workers also misuse sick leave or use alcohol and drugs on the job.

The American Heritage Dictionary defines *honest* as "absolutely genuine, having integrity, honorable, not lying, cheating, or taking an unfair advantage."

You can't be truly successful *and* dishonest. Winston Churchill said, "It's important to be honest, but it's also important to be right." It is no more "right" to steal time from your employer than it is to steal from the cash register. It's old and trite, but it's still true and right. Honesty is not just the best policy, it is the *only* policy.

Action Steps

1. Today I will do what is *right,* no matter how difficult it may seem.
2. Today I will_____

_____

Prefer loss to the wealth of dishonest gain; the former vexes you for a time; the latter will bring you lasting remorse.

Chilo

. . . and Followers

*L*eaders are sorely needed, but here's a pretty good case for followers.

A young woman wanted to go to college in a story told by S. I. McMillen in his book, *None of These Diseases*. But her heart sank when she read the question on the application blank which asked, "Are you a leader?" Being both honest and conscientious, she wrote "no" and returned the application expecting the worst.

To her surprise, she received this letter from the college: "Dear Applicant: A study of the application forms reveals that this year our college will have 1,452 new leaders. We are accepting you because we feel it is imperative that they have at least *one* follower!"

"It's a pity," Dr. McMillen says, "that we race each other like participants in a stock car race. In our excitement to be first, we ignore the damage we inflict on others and ourselves."

A man once prayed, "Lord, keep me from becoming so self-possessed that I must express myself on every subject. With my vast store of wisdom, it *does* seem a *pity* not to use it all, but Thou knowest, Lord, that I want to have a few friends at the end."

One way to become a leader is to study leaders and *follow* their examples.

Action Steps

1. Today I will *follow* the example of good leaders so that when my opportunity to lead comes, I will be prepared.
2. Today I will_____

Who hath not served cannot command.

John Florio

21

. . . and Persuasion

A study at Yale University recently revealed something that good sales people have known for a long time. After weeks of testing the appearances, personalities, and attitudes of subjects and their influence on others, the professors at Yale have discovered that a *smile* is the single most powerful force of influence that we have. That's good news because we can always provide smiles.

However, you must do more than smile if you are going to be successful in influencing other people to take action. For example, you must get across your message in an understandable and believable manner. If you're going to make the sale, communication experts say you must repeat the message three times without being obvious that you are repeating yourself. I'll say it again, you must repeat your message at least three times to make it clear. Repetition is the mother of learning and a powerful tool.

The final point is one that is equally simple and one that most of us have known for a long time. The third most important factor in influencing others is sincerity and honesty. It shouldn't require a university study to convince us that sincerity and honesty are important.

A warm, friendly smile, persistence with your message, and a show of sincerity and honesty is a tough combination to beat, whether you are selling a product, seeking a job, or trying to win a seat on the school board.

Action Steps

1. Today I will smile sincerely at *all* those with whom I come in contact.
2. Today I will combine persistence with honesty, and I will succeed!
3. Today I will_____

_____

> *You can only make others better by being good yourself.*
>
> Hugh R. Haweis

. . . and Limitations

*H*e was rated "dull, slow, and impractical" by his teachers and was asked to leave college. Despite this negative start, he was awarded a patent for the rotary steam engine before he turned twenty. His next invention, a device that put derailed trains back on the track, was purchased by virtually every railroad in the country. Before this man's creative life was over, he patented over four hundred inventions and amassed an industrial empire that few have equalled.

Even though he was disabled near the end of his life, he continued to invent, using his wheelchair to transport him from one project to another. He died surrounded by the sketches of his latest project—the motorized wheelchair.

The man labeled as "impractical and dull" was named George Westinghouse. He refused to accept the negative opinions of those around him and instead chose to become one of the richest and most creative men in history. I hope you choose to believe in yourself and strive for your goals even if others express negative opinions of your abilities.

Action Steps

1. Today I will refuse to accept negative and limiting comments.
2. Today I will_____

_____

> *Genius is one percent inspiration and ninety-nine percent perspiration.*
> Thomas A. Edison

. . . and Youth

I'm proud of America's youth. I believe America's youth are our country's richest resource. The publishers of *Who's Who Among American High School Students* conducted a tenth anniversary survey in 1980 to determine attitudes and values among America's student leaders. Twenty-three thousand leading high school juniors and seniors were surveyed. I'd like to share some of their opinions with you. I think you'll be as impressed as I was:

Seventy percent had set clear career goals

Seventy-four percent did not approve legalizing marijuana

Ninety-two percent did not use marijuana

Seventy-eight percent had not participated in premarital sex

Eighty-six percent were members of organized religion

Seventy-five percent felt that religion played a significant role in their lives

Eighty-five percent preferred traditional marriage.

These are the answers from students chosen as the outstanding high school students in our nation. When you think about it for a moment, it's easy to understand why these students are in *Who's Who.* By avoiding pot they have full control of their faculties and don't have to worry about getting stoned and killing somebody with a car. Faith gives them peace of mind. By abstaining from premarital sex they eliminate the possibility of venereal disease or unwanted pregnancy. In short, these young people can concentrate on being good students, growing up, and setting lifetime goals.

These students think for themselves. They have the healthiest self-images and the clearest picture of what they want in life. A part of having a healthy self-image is being able to clearly state "This is who I am and this is where I'm heading."

Action Steps

1. Today I will take time to think about "who I am" and "where I'm heading."

2. Today I will_____

_____

> *He that respects himself is safe from others; he wears a coat of mail that none can pierce.*
>
> Henry Wadsworth Longfellow

. . . and Challenges

*T*om Dempsey kicked a sixty-three-yard field goal for the New Orleans Saints. It's one of the longest field goals in the history of the NFL. That in itself is admirable, but what makes this feat even more exciting is that Tom Dempsey kicked that field goal with a foot half the size of his other one. Tom was born with a right foot that has no toes.

Tom gives credit to his parents for overcoming his handicap. He puts it this way: "I was lucky. I had parents who didn't put limitations on me because of my problem. When it came to physical tests, they *never told me I couldn't*. I was taught that a handicap was a challenge and not an excuse, so whatever I decided to try as a boy, I did." If you meet life's challenges with an "I-think-I-can" attitude as Tom Dempsey did, you have a huge head start over those who are afraid of failure.

Wally Piper's classic, "The Little Engine that Could," is about a little blue engine asked in an emergency to pull the freight train over the mountain. The engine had never been over the mountain but it thought it could and believed it could—and it succeeded. We all have handicaps of some type. But Tom Dempsey's half-foot didn't stop *him* from kicking hundreds of field goals—including a sixty-three yarder. I hope you'll see your handicaps and problems as challenges and not excuses.

Action Steps

1. Today I will use only positive "self-talk"; like the little engine, "I think I can" will be my motto.
2. Today I will_____

_____

When a man has put a limit on what he will do, he has put a limit on what he can do.

Charles M. Schwab

. . . and Growth

*H*e was sickly and skinny during high school, the proverbial "ninety-seven-pound weakling." He wore thick glasses, arch supports, and a shoulder brace. He was so self-conscious about his appearance that he dropped out of school.

His future looked bleak. Then one day he attended a health lecture and decided that he wanted his future to be different from his past. So he began to exercise two hours each day. He changed his junk food diet. Slowly he changed his appearance, self-image, and future. The change was so great that he opened up one of the first health studios in the United States. He went door-to-door in Oakland, California, promoting his new exercise business.

For over forty-seven years now, he has promoted exercise. His reputation has spread nationally and then internationally. Many think of him as "Mr. Exercise." He now has his own private gym and drives an eighty-thousand-dollar car. He attributes his success to his ability to change the course of his life when he was a teenager. His name is Jack LaLanne.

Jack LaLanne will be the first to tell you that his change of direction wasn't easy. It won't be easy for you either, but your future can be different from your past. It's up to you.

Action Steps

1. Today I will take responsibility for my own destiny.
2. Today I will_____

_____

A man has to live with himself, and he should see to it that he always has good company.

Charles Evans Hughes

. . . and Details

*I*n the game of life, it's not the major things which often determine success or failure, happiness or misery—it's the little things. The clock which is four hours wrong is not a problem. We instantly know it's wrong and make the correction. However, the one which is four minutes wrong is another matter.

In my case, if my watch is four minutes slow I usually can't identify it as a problem. I fly a lot, and if my watch loses just a few minutes I might arrive at 2:34 to catch a 2:30 plane. This can be disastrous! (I have a deal with the airlines that if I'm not there when they get ready to go, they are to go ahead without me. Recently in Dallas I found out that the airlines live up to their end of the agreement!) I also have discovered that airplanes are easier to catch *before* they leave the ground.

Little things make a difference. Call a girl a kitten and she'll love you. Call her a cat and you have an entirely different matter. Say she's a vision and score points; tell her she's a sight and you're in trouble!

Yes, little things *do* make a big difference! If you will take care of the "little things," then the "big things" will automatically fall into place for you.

Action Steps

1. Today I will have a kind word for someone who is unable to help me.
2. Today I will_____

_____

When you are good to others you are best to yourself.

Dr. Louis L. Mann

. . . and Consistency

*C*onsistency in discipline is important whether you're talking about punishment, chores, recreation, or values. Christian psychologist Henry Brandt was asked if parents should make their children attend church. His reply was, "Yes." Dr. Brandt points out that if a child is sick you take him to the doctor whether or not he wants to go because it's good for him. You take him to church for the same reason.

"Are you startled? Why? How do you answer ten-year-old Junior when he comes to breakfast and announces that he isn't going to school anymore? How do you answer him when he says, 'I'm not going to take a bath'? Junior bathes, doesn't he?

"Why all this timidity, then, in the realm of his spiritual guidance? Are you going to wait and let him decide what church he will go to when he is old enough? Quit kidding. You didn't wait until he was old enough to decide whether he wishes to remain dirty or clean. Do you decide if he is old enough to decide if he wants to take medicine when he is sick? So, what will you say when Junior says he does not like to go to church? That's easy to answer. *Just be consistent.*"

Consistency in parental discipline and example are important whether you're talking about punishment, chores, recreation, or values. And values are the capstone of the disciplinary process. As psychologist James Dobson expresses it, "Values are not taught, they're caught."

Action Steps

1. Today I will be *consistent* in my dealings with others.
2. Today I will_____

_____

All children are born good.

Lord Palmerston

29

. . . and Worry

*A*re you a worrier? Americans take more pills to forget more worries about more silly things than ever before. Why is worry your enemy? Because *worry will destroy you*. According to Dr. Charles Mayo, "Worry affects the circulation and the whole nervous system. I have never known a man who died from overwork, but many who died from doubt."

Psychologists tell us that forty percent of our worries will *never happen* and that thirty percent have *already happened*. An additional twelve percent of our worries are over unfounded health concerns; ten percent more involve the daily miscellaneous fretting that accomplishes absolutely nothing. Now if my addition is right, that leaves only eight percent. In other words, those who study the field of worry have discovered that Americans are worrying ninety-two percent of the time for no good reason. And if Dr. Charles Mayo is right, it's killing us.

Here's a suggestion. Don't worry about what you can't change. Instead, *use* that energy in a positive, productive way. If you don't like your state in life, don't stew or worry about it, do something about it. Worry less and act more, because worry, like the rocking chair, won't take you anywhere.

Action Steps

1. Today I will make a list of my ten greatest worries and will compare them to Dr. Mayo's formula.
2. Today I will_____

_____

Worry is worship to the wrong god.

Jack Exum

. . . and Sunshine

*W*orthington Industry began twenty-eight years ago with one person, John McConnell. The company has experienced phenomenal growth; today Worthington has revenues of five hundred million dollars.

McConnell has been so successful that executives frequently visit his plants to discover his secret of success. McConnell says his operating manual can be summed up in the Golden Rule: "Do unto others as you would have then do unto you." That is, treat others like you want to be treated.

As McConnell says, "We are a Golden Rule company. To me, that's the way to live—for everybody. The idea is that if you can reverse your thinking and see things from the other person's standpoint—although it's sometimes difficult to do—the problems will disappear." That simple philosophy has turned Worthington into a huge success. At a time when many investors are selling steel stocks, Worthington stockholders are keeping theirs.

I applaud John McConnell for his philosophy. I happen to believe it is the soundest personal and business philosophy a man or woman can possess. You see, I believe you can achieve anything you want in life if you help enough other people get what *they* want in life.

Action Steps

1. Today I will treat my family, business associates, and strangers with the same attitude with which I would like to be treated.
2. Today I will_____

_____

Those who bring sunshine into the lives of others cannot keep it from themselves.
James M. Barrie

31

. . . and Honesty

*J*ohn Morley once traveled from England to Canada to address the graduating class of a university. He began his speech by saying, "I have traveled four thousand miles to tell you that there is a difference between right and wrong."

If a man has a two-hundred-thousand-dollar house but goes to jail for cheating on his income taxes, he has failed to appreciate the difference between right and wrong. If a wife promises to be faithful to her husband and then breaks that trust, she has failed to appreciate the difference between right and wrong. If parents tell their children to tell a salesman that they're not at home, they've failed to appreciate the difference between right and wrong. If a son agrees to drive the car straight to school and back, and doesn't do it, he's failed to appreciate the difference between right and wrong. If a girl lies to her parents about where she went on a date, she's failed to appreciate the difference between right and wrong.

Dr. Mortimer Feinberg, author of *Corporate Bigamy,* interviewed one hundred top executives with Fortune 500 companies. These men said that anyone who thinks he can get to the top and stay there without honesty is dumb. That's strong, *and* it's accurate.

Building a life on genuineness and honesty includes practicing the difference between right and wrong.

Action Steps

1. Today I will do what I know to be right, regardless of the short-term discomfort.
2. Today I will_____

No individual has the right to determine what law shall be obeyed and what law shall be enforced.

Herbert Hoover

. . . and Courage

*F*or the average high school defensive back, intercepting four passes in five games is pretty good. For Randy Waters, it's astounding. Now add punts of an average of nearly forty yards and extra points as well. Randy is also the number-one doubles player and number-two singles player on the school's tennis team. Despite all the time he spends with sports activities, he maintains an A-minus average in the classroom.

If we stopped the story at this point, it would be a good one, but we are just getting started—or should I say that Randy is just getting started? He is also planning a college athletic career.

Here's what's so special about all of this. Four years ago, as Randy tells the story, "I got my shirtsleeve caught in a meat grinder and it just pulled me on in. After that, well, it was an uphill battle. For a while I thought about just lying down and dying. Tina Sherrill and Lumpkin County, Georgia, High School Coach Bobby Rich gave me a chance to keep playing football." The rest of the story is that Randy performs his heroics with one arm and hand, plus a tremendous positive attitude. He doesn't look down at what he lost; he concentrates on what he *has* and determines to use it to the fullest. That attitude makes Randy a winner and it'll do the same for you.

Action Steps

1. Today I will tell two people the story of Randy Waters so that it might inspire them and serve as a reminder to me.
2. Today I will_____

_____

Courage is the first of human qualities because it is the quality that guarantees all others.

Sir Winston Churchill

. . . and Hope

*T*he doctor was wrong, but Harry Perry was even more wrong. He was told he was dying of leukemia, so he threw in the towel and started to act as if life was over. He quit his job, ruled out marriage, spent thousands on treatments, drank heavily, and spent most of his time alone. He was waiting to die, but he might as well have been dead already. Harry's life was empty, even though he wasn't dead—as a matter of fact, he wasn't even dying.

About five years after the initial diagnosis, another checkup showed that Harry did *not* have the disease. He has since then married, bought a home, and quit treatments. He feels great.

Nothing has actually changed except Harry's *attitude*. When he thought he was dying, he set a course of self-destruction. When he learned he wasn't a victim of leukemia, he set a course of living and fulfillment. The tragedy is that all of the potential characteristics of happiness and success were there all the time; he simply stopped using them. You have them, too, if you will use them. Don't let your epitaph read, "Born 1950, Died 1984, Buried 1999."

Action Steps

1. Today I will remember that I am "born to win"; my attitude will reflect my confidence.
2. Today I will _____

_____

> *Whatever happens, do not lose hold on the two main ropes of life—hope and faith.*

. . . and Influence

"We gave up entirely too much in dealing with the Chinese and the Russians."

I listened with interest because the voice and the words were familiar as the speaker talked about how the Russians and the Chinese had "done us in" at the negotiating table. The voice, you see, was that of my fourteen-year-old son, as he was talking to the passenger in the seat next to him on a recent flight.

I was certainly pleased that my son was interested in foreign affairs, and was delighted that he was quoting his dad. Then it hit me full force: the responsibility we as parents have is tremendous, because our children often become our echoes. We are, in fact, the role models for our children; they walk in our footsteps. Many times our morals and values become their morals and values.

Our children become miniature reproductions of us. So the question for the parent is: What kind of role model are you? Will you be proud to look back and say, "My child has walked in my footsteps"? I hope so, because your child and my child make up the future of America.

Action Steps

1. Today I will realize the responsibility that I have to my fellow man to set the proper example.
2. Today I will_____

_____

I don't know who my grandfather was; I am much more concerned to know what his grandson will be.

Abraham Lincoln

... the Fine Line

*M*ost of us will never collect one of the big, prestigious prizes—the Pulitzer, the Nobel, the Oscar, or Tony, or Emmy—that are reserved for an elite few. For example, every child born in this country in this day theoretically has an opportunity to become president of the United States. But the simple fact is that most will miss that elusive prize.

All of us, however, *are* eligible for life's small pleasures. Anyone can treasure a pat on the back, a hug, a kiss, a four-pound bass, a full moon, or an empty parking space—right by the door! Those small pleasures can include a crackling log in the fireplace, iced tea, hot soup, or a beautiful sunset. Even greater "simple" enjoyments are available: the opportunity to realize the freedom to travel, to vote for whomever we please, or to worship in the synagogue or church of our choice. All of these and a thousand other things give each one of us a lot of things to be grateful for and provide each of us with a constant source of delight.

If life's greatest awards come your way, be grateful. And if they pass you by, don't fret. Enjoy the small delights that life offers. Yesterday's heroes are today's forgotten people; life's big prizes are singular events, soon forgotten. But life's little treasures go on and on. Today may not be full of great pleasures, but it can be full of little ones. You need only open your eyes and look around.

Action Steps

1. Today I will enjoy the "small victories" and life's little pleasures by recognizing the joy they contain.
2. Today I will_____

If you consistently do your best, the worst won't happen.

B. C. Forbes

. . . and Warm Fuzzies

*Y*ou have probably heard the term *positive strokes* (some people use the expression *warm fuzzies*). It doesn't matter what term you use, but it is important for you to do your part in spreading positive feelings wherever you go. Make it a habit to compliment co-workers, friends, and family members for well-done jobs. Look beneath the surface in apparently negative situations and find something positive to say. This will take effort and ingenuity on your part, but when you pay sincere compliments and show honest appreciation for the talents of another person, the rewards will be well worth the effort.

I've discovered that one of the very best ways to maintain a happy and healthy attitude each day is by helping someone else to do the same thing. The moment I *give* a positive stroke, I *get* in return the warm fuzzies. Every time I *sincerely* compliment someone on a job well done, I feel warm inside. So if you haven't gotten your positive strokes today, maybe it's because you haven't given any out.

Action Steps

1. Today I will *sincerely* compliment co-workers, friends, and family members for well-done jobs. In particular I want to find something positive to say about _____ , _____ _____ and _____ .
2. Today I will_____
   _____

The surest way to knock the chip off a fellow's shoulder is by patting him on the back.

. . . and Prison

*D*o you believe it's possible for a man or woman to make a change from being a prison inmate to become a successful businessman? I do, and Larry Wells of Expedition Outreach is living proof that it can happen.

For many people a fifteen-year prison term would be an impossible barrier to overcome. But Larry Wells proved to be a man of determination and deep faith in the power of the positive over the negative.

Larry spent fifteen years in the Idaho State Prison for armed robbery. But a very simple thing happened that changed his entire life, which in turn has changed the lives of hundreds of young men. Larry's parents never gave up on their son. They sent him a copy of James Allen's book, *As a Man Thinketh,* which hit Larry like a thunderbolt when he read it. It convinced him that you are exactly what you think you are. From that day forward Larry Wells got rid of his "stinkin' thinkin'" and began to practice positive thinking.

Today, Larry is head of Expedition Outreach, a program that establishes a positive self-image in the minds of young men. Larry Wells proved you can change your life by changing your thinking. It worked for him and it will work for you.

Action Steps

1. Today I will remember the adage "As a man thinketh in his heart, so is he" and I will hold tight to the good thoughts in my mind and heart!
2. Today I will_____

_____

There's nothing either good or bad, but thinking makes it so.

Shakespeare

. . . and "Stinkin' Thinkin' "

*Y*our business is never good or bad "out there." It is good or bad right between your ears.

Many years ago, while speaking at a Board of Realtors meeting in Flint, Michigan, I was visiting pleasantly with a real estate salesman when I made the mistake of asking him about his business. I expected enthusiasm, but I got a long dissertation on how bad business was since General Motors was on strike. He pointed out that people were holding onto every dime and were buying only the absolute necessities. His attitude was so negative he could have brightened up the room only by leaving it!

Someone diverted his attention for a moment and I quickly turned to the little lady on my right and asked her, "Well, how's everything?" She responded, "Well, you know, Mr. Ziglar, General Motors is on strike." I thought to myself, "Oh, no, not again!" Then she broke into a beautiful smile and gave me a long list of reasons why that was good for her business. She ended by asking if I knew anyone in Washington. When I asked her why she wanted to know, she responded, "If I could just keep this strike going for another six weeks, I could take the rest of the year off!"

One person was going broke because of the strike. Another person in the same business was getting rich because of the strike. The difference? Attitude! "Stinkin' thinkin' " has no place in your business or your life.

Action Steps

1. Today I will eliminate "stinkin' thinkin' " by looking for the good that can come out of every situation.
2. Today I will_____

There exist limitless opportunities in every industry. Where there is an open mind, there will always be a frontier.

Charles F. Kettering

... and Law

*L*aw enforcement is not an easy job, but occasionally there are humorous moments that brighten an officer's day.

If you've driven a car for very long it's very likely that on some rare occasion you've exceeded the speed limit and heard the sound of authority from behind you. And if you're like the rest of us, you've tried to come up with a quick alibi—like the nervous man in Missouri who said, "I was just keeping up with the cars behind me." Or the young lady who had a slight accident and said, "I was coming home, pulled into the wrong driveway, and hit a tree I don't have." Another man once said, "I drove my car for forty years and finally fell asleep at the wheel and ran into the ditch."

Some motorists exhibit real ingenuity in their efforts to avoid the inevitable ticket, but generally speaking the offending motorist loses the discussion. One creative patrolman takes some sting out of the process and writes only "courtesy tickets"—meaning that he is real courteous when he hands them out. Law enforcement men of America, we thank you for being so understanding, and for doing a great job.

Action Steps

1. Today I will thank a law enforcement officer (in person, by phone, or by letter) for his commitment.
2. Today I will_____

Wherever law ends, tyranny begins.

John Locke

. . . and Ingenuity

*W*hen we think of success we often think of Henry Ford and the assembly line or J. C. Penney and his line of retail stores. Yes, these men were extremely successful and lived the American dream. But there are hundreds and thousands of people who live their own American dream in a much different way.

Dennis Koepsell looked around for an opportunity that would combine his love for selling and his interest in history and antiques. He had no idea what he was looking for until the day he came across an old worn-out antique popcorn wagon. Now for most of us it would have remained an old, worn-out popcorn wagon. But Dennis saw something in that old wagon that most of us probably would have overlooked.

After months and months of painstaking restoration work, Dennis was able to get the wagon into working order. He popped old-fashioned popcorn at special events around his home town. It wasn't long before he bought another one and then another. Today Dennis Koepsell is the "Popcorn King" of Milwaukee. He now has six wagons working full time and has plans for four more.

That's American ingenuity. That's the American dream. Chances are excellent that you are just as smart as Dennis Koepsell. The difference could be that Dennis kept his eyes open and recognized that opportunity often comes dressed up in hard work.

Action Steps

1. Today I will be more aware of the opportunities all around me.
2. Today I will_____

_____

We need men who can dream of things that never were.
John F. Kennedy

... and Comparison

I'm a proud parent and I have eagerly joined in the conversations of friends and family as we discussed the progress of our little ones. It seems that whenever progress of children is discussed, however, comparison with others comes up. James Dobson points out that most of us compare our children in two areas: physical appearance and intelligence. Dr. Dobson explains that this can cause serious self-image problems in children. For a child, this comparison can lead to the idea that if he doesn't look like the person on the latest magazine cover or doesn't have an impressive I.Q. score, he is an inferior human being.

But every person is important! No one else can bring the same joy and delight to that mom or dad, that husband or wife, that brother or sister, that you, who are loved *because you are you,* can bring. You are unique and special. No one else can make *your* contribution to mankind. There's no need for comparison but only for cultivation of your unique qualities.

Action Steps

1. Today I will believe in myself and will not compare my worst features to someone else's best features.
2. Today I will_____

> *'Tis looking downward makes one dizzy.*
>
> Robert Browning

42

. . . and Capacity

I believe man was designed for accomplishment, engineered for success, and endowed with the seeds of greatness. That includes *you*. You are a valuable person, capable of great things.

However, if you've heard all of your life that you don't measure up, chances are good you believe it. If you've been repeatedly told that you have to win approval, you'll try to win it. If you're told daily that you are second rate, you just might begin to agree. That, my friend, is known as garbage-dump thinking and can be disastrous. For example, evangelist Bill Glass has learned through his prison ministry that approximately ninety percent of all inmates had been repeatedly told by their parents that they would end up in jail!

Tom Mullen, in his book, *Seriously, Life Is a Laughing Matter,* tells of a fifteen-year-old girl named Amy who had always received straight *A* s in school. Her parents were extremely upset when she received a *B*. "If I fail in what I do," Amy said in a note to her parents, "I fail in what I am." That message was part of Amy's suicide note. Input into the mind ultimately influences our behavior.

It is sad that Amy is far from being an unusual case. The number of teenage suicides in the United States has tripled in the last decade to over *thirty a day*. Americans have been fed a lot of garbage. It's not what you do or have, it's what you are that's important. It's not disgraceful to fail—the disgrace is in refusing to try.

You are capable of great things. Use the ability you have and you'll be given more ability to use.

Action Steps

1. Today I will use what I have to do what I can.
2. Today I will _____

Be careful of your thoughts. They may break into words at any time.

. . . and Words

*T*he word that could determine your success in life has only three letters: it is *can*. The word *can* is one of the most powerful words in the English language. In fact, as you may know, we've developed the "I Can" course to accentuate the power of believing in your ability to reach your goals.

Ironically, the addition of the letter *t* to the word *can* means the difference between success and failure. Historians say that significant achievements in America were made in spite of the word *can't*. For example, these statements are taken directly from newspapers:

Anyone traveling at the speed of thirty miles per hour will definitely suffocate (1840).

No possible combination can be united into a practical machine by which men shall fly (1901).

The foolish idea of shooting at the moon is basically impossible (1926).

To harness the energy locked up in matter is impossible (1930).

I'm glad men like Edison and the Wright Brothers didn't accept the word *can't*. I hope *you* will substitute the word *can* for *can't*. It's only the difference of a letter, but it can change your performance in life.

Action Steps

1. Today I will remove the word *can't* from my vocabulary and substitute *won't* or *don't know how*—or *can*.
2. Today I will_____

_____

Words, like glasses, obscure everything which they do not make clear.
Joseph Joubert

... and Impossibilities

I am continuously amazed at the abilities of athletes who run faster, jump higher, and execute feats of physical skill with greater precision every year. Every day we read about a young athlete who cracks a barrier.

The most famous athletic barrier was the four-minute mile. Experts believed for many years that it was impossible for a human being to run a mile in under four minutes. But in 1954, a man named Roger Bannister ran the mile in less than four minutes. Today, high school athletes and a thirty-seven-year-old man have accomplished that remarkable feat.

There was a time when experts believed a twenty-eight-foot long jump was physically impossible, but Bob Beamon pulled off one of the most incredible athletic achievements of our time when he went right on past the twenty-eight-foot marker and jumped twenty-nine feet. Nadia Comaneci broke the "ten" barrier in the 1976 Olympic Games and now several girls have gone on to score perfect tens in gymnastic competition.

Isn't it amazing that when one person breaks the barrier others quickly follow them to the top? Often the only limits that we have are those we place upon ourselves. Once we clearly understand that the "barriers" are mental limitations and not physical impossibilities, our chances of improving performance and breaking those records are dramatically improved. As a matter of fact, when we *realize* something can be done, you can bet it *will* be done.

Action Steps

1. Today I will remove my limitations by realizing that although others can stop me temporarily, I am the only one who can stop myself permanently.
2. Today I will_____

_____

Impossible is a word to be found only in the dictionary of fools.
                                                    Napoleon Bonaparte

---

... Insignificant Incidents

*O*pportunity is often the result of accidental discoveries. For example, the first smoke alarm was the result of an insignificant incident in a laboratory. Duane Pearsall was testing an electronic device that controls static electricity when he noticed that the smoke from a technician's cigarette caused the meter in the device to go bad. At first, Pearsall was irritated that he had to stop the experiment and get a new meter installed. Later he realized that the reaction of the meter to smoke might prove to be a valuable bit of information. That brief and seemingly insignificant accident led to Pearsall's production of the first American-made smoke detector alarm system, a system that has saved thousands of lives.

Success can come in many ways. Sometimes it's the result of what appears to be an insignificant incident. Get in the habit of looking for opportunities—stretch your mind, look for possibilities. They exist everywhere and are frequently under our very noses.

Action Steps

1. Today I will look a second time at all the seemingly insignificant incidents that are actually opportunities that present themselves around me.
2. Today I will_____

_____

Many do with opportunities as children do at the sea shore; they fill their little hands with sand, and then let the grains fall through, one by one, till all are gone.

. . . and the Winning Ingredients

*W*hat is the most important ingredient college coaches look for in high school athletes? Each spring college coaches spend hours of time visiting with high school sportsmen. Recently, one of the top college coaches was asked this question: "What is the winning ingredient you are looking for in a young athlete?"

The coach replied without hesitation, "We are looking for young men who will accept coaching."

Successful coaches know that individuals with physical skill alone will not guarantee a winning team. They know that each player on the team must be willing to take constructive criticism and to accept instruction so that they can blend in with the other players and become a team.

Each of us must be willing to accept criticism. We must learn to listen to the advice of experts. No matter how competent we think we are in a certain job, we can always find room for improvement.

Can you take coaching? Would you be a prospect for a championship team? Do you fully understand that every person on the company payroll plays an important part in the overall success of the business? In order for you to be a champion on a championship team, you need to remain open to advice and coaching.

Action Steps

1. Today I will seek out championship performers, and I will seek advice and counsel from them.
2. Today I will_____

_____

He that walketh with wise men shall be wise.

Proverbs 13 : 20

. . . and Age

*Y*ou've heard the statement many times that this is a young person's world—and a quick check of the history books rapidly establishes that this statement has considerable validity. For example, Lindberg at age twenty-five was the first man to fly nonstop over the Atlantic Ocean to Paris; John Paul Jones was a full sea captain at twenty-two; Napoleon was an artillery captain before he was twenty-three; Edgar Allen Poe was internationally known as a poet at eighteen; Tracy Austin won the U.S. Open Tennis Championship at age sixteen; Alexander the Great had conquered the known world at twenty-six; Eli Whitney was twenty-eight when he perfected the cotton gin. We also frequently see stories of child prodigies who at age five are solving mathematical equations that confound college professors. The list is truly endless of all the people who've done remarkable things before their thirtieth birthday.

This obviously proves that it is a young person's world. Or does it? I'm going to prove that it's also an old person's or even a middle-aged person's world. As a matter of fact, it is really *your* world, regardless of your age. Read on and you'll see what I mean.

Commodore Vanderbilt was not known as a great railroad king until he was seventy; at eighty-eight he was the most active railroad man of his day. Socrates started studying music when he was eighty; Pasteur discovered his hydrophobia cure when he was sixty; Columbus was well over fifty when he made his first voyage of American discovery; Voltaire, Newton, Spencer, Talleyrand, and Thomas Jefferson all were active and in their intellectual prime after eighty. Grandma Moses achieved her fame and success after age ninety. Galileo discovered the monthly and daily phases of the moon when he was seventy-three. The list is endless.

What this really says is that the world belongs to anybody who will recognize that now is the time and here is the place—to go to the top.

Action Steps

1. Today I will realize that age is not an obstacle or barrier, but is an asset.
2. Today I will_____

_____

48

To me, old age is always fifteen years older than I am.
Bernard M. Baruch

. . . and Enthusiasm

*I*nstant enthusiasm is available. If you want to develop instant enthusiasm, simply reverse the way you get out of bed! No, don't get out backwards, but neither should you get out moaning about another bad day.

I have some good news and some bad news about this. The bad news is first: you'll feel foolish following the procedure I'm going to describe. The good news is that you'll get more living out of life—and maybe even earn more money—by doing this. You may not get fat checks in the mail right away, but you'll earn more by being more productive and shortly you'll receive the benefits.

Here's what you do. Tomorrow when you hear the sound of the "opportunity clock" (negative folks call it an "alarm clock"), sit straight up in bed, clap your hands, and say, "Oh, boy, it's a great day to get out and take advantage of the opportunities the world has to offer!" Now, you might feel ridiculous and you will probably look silly, since your hair will probably be down in your face and you might still be half-asleep, but you will be up—and that's where you wanted to be when you set the opportunity clock! Chances are good that you will be laughing at yourself, but laughter is a sure sign of enthusiasm, and laughing at yourself shows a healthy self-image. Results are guaranteed. Try it every day for twenty-one days and I will see you at the top!

Action Steps

1. Today I will get up with enthusiasm by clapping my hands and saying, "Oh, boy, it's a great day to get out and take advantage of the opportunities the world has to offer!"
2. Today I will_____

Enthusiasm is the greatest asset in the world. It beats money and power and influence.

Henry Chester

. . . and Television

*D*o people take what they view on television too seriously? The answer is "yes." For example, several years ago on "The Edge of Night," two of the leading characters got married. The details of the wedding were so real and so complete that 576 gifts were received as wedding presents from the viewing audience. Some were minor and insignificant, but a number of them involved substantial expense.

Not too long ago at a prayer meeting, one dear lady stood up and asked for special prayer for a friend of hers. Later it was learned that this "special friend" was a character in a soap opera. In my judgment this fantasy, which is portrayed so convincingly on television, can lead to serious problems. Not only are these programs time-consuming, but the fantasy removes a person from the reality of building his own life.

Give yourself this little test: how upset do you get when an unexpected visitor pops in while you are viewing your favorite program or soap opera? If you really get upset, you are too involved in that imaginary world and not enough involved in your own real world. Think about it. From my perspective, I'm convinced that it is *impossible* to view the soaps on a daily basis and maintain an optimistic, moral attitude about life.

Action Steps

1. Today I will control my own life and not allow the television set to exert control.
2. Today I will_____

_____

Temperance is moderation in the things that are good and total abstinence from the things that are foul.

Frances E. Willard

51

... "Go" Lights

*T*o build enthusiasm, go to the "go" lights. Here's what I mean. In our negative society, most people talk about stop lights, weekends, and colds. My brother-friend from Winnipeg, Canada, Bernie Lofchick, has a different vocabulary. He has never had a cold—that's negative. He occasionally does have a "warm," though. With him, Saturdays and Sundays are not weekends, they are "strong-ends." He does not encounter stop lights, they are "go" lights.

A good step in building enthusiasm is to use a positive vocabulary. In all fairness I must point out that you can survive without a positive vocabulary, but I'm not talking about mere survival. I'm talking about enthusiasm for life and having more fun while building a better future.

Incidentally, this approach is realistic and practical. The "go" lights do make traffic go faster and more safely. You rest on Saturday and Sunday, so you will get strong for the next week. When your temperature goes up, you have caught a "warm." So get enthusiastic by talking about "go" lights, "warms," and "strong-ends." Incidentally, this will bring smiles to lots of faces, smiles that will help build enthusiasm for everyone. Try it. You'll like it!

Action Steps

1. Today I will bring up "go" lights in conversations and will watch the smiles I help create.
2. Today I will_____

_____

Nothing great was ever accomplished without enthusiasm.

. . . and You

*W*ill Rogers never spoke for ten years.

It will undoubtedly come as a tremendous shock to large numbers of people, but Will Rogers—who is considered by many to be the greatest folk philosopher-humorist of this century—never said a single word from the stage during the first ten years of his professional life. Will Rogers was a cowboy—a rope-trick artist and man's man of incredible skill. He performed feats of wizardry and magic with the rope for the first ten years of his career, but he never uttered a word. An impromptu situation occurred at one of the performances and Will made a comment. The audience responded and Will Rogers—the philosopher-humorist—was on his way.

Perhaps one of the greatest things he ever said was, "If you want to succeed in life, you've got to know what you're doing, believe in what you're doing, and love what you're doing." That's a marvelous formula for success for anyone.

Do you know what you are doing? Do you believe in what you are doing? Do you love what you are doing? If you do, then you really are on your way to the top!

Action Steps

1. Today I will take time to consider the personal benefits in my activities—how I know, believe in, and love what I am doing.
2. Today I will_____

_____

The reward of a thing well done is to have done it.

Ralph Waldo Emerson

53

. . . and Small Tasks

*T*his quote from *Reader's Digest* says a lot: "Whoever thinks he is too important for small tasks is probably too small for important ones."

Today many of our young people have the unrealistic expectation of landing the perfect lifetime job (the one that is rewarding, exciting, challenging, well-paying, and has a "future") on the first try. That kind of thinking taken too literally can be disastrous. In most cases, the first job doesn't and simply can't offer that much. Employers are far more inclined to hire you for the ideal job if you are already doing a good job working on a less-than-ideal job.

So young people, if that first job is honest and doesn't compromise your moral principles (like causing you to sell booze, work on Sunday, or work in a place that sells pornography), take it. Then give that job everything you've got! From there you can either move up or out to that ideal job with a future. So go ahead, get started, and after a lot of persistence and hard work with the right mental attitude, I'll see *you* at the top!

Action Steps

1. Today I will do every task with the same enthusiasm that is normally reserved for major projects.
2. Today I will_____

The fellow who is fired with enthusiasm for his boss is seldom fired by the boss.

. . . and Energy

*I*n the vast majority of cases, our physical tiredness is not really a physical problem; we are simply suffering from mental exhaustion, sometimes known as "stinkin' thinkin'." Here's an example (you men who read this will relate to this example better than the ladies).

The day has been one of "those" days, all day long, and everything that could go wrong has gone wrong. One frustrating event has piled on top of yet another frustrating event. At the end of the day, you stagger home, too tired to put one foot in front of the other.

Your wife greets you cheerfully and enthusiastically, expressing her delight in the fact that you are not late in getting home, since this is "the" day. You wearily inquire, "What day?" Your wife eagerly responds that this is the day that six weeks ago you had set aside to clean the garage. You feebly protest that you cannot put one foot in front of the other. Your wife promises to help but again you deny the presence of any energy.

However, at that precise instant the telephone rings and the voice at the other end says to you, "Hey, pardner, I've got a tee time at the country club in fifteen minutes. We still have time to get in nine holes before dark, if you can make it." All of a sudden the tiredness disappears and you enthusiastically respond that you'll be there in *ten* minutes.

In one form or another, the above example recurs millions of times every day. The point is simple: when you reinforce your feeling of tiredness by acknowledging it, you further reduce your energy reserve. Visualize yourself enjoying the task, and you'll be amazed at how much more energy you have.

Action Steps

1. Today, *every time* I am asked, "How are you?," I will respond with "Super good, but I'll get better!"
2. Today I will_____
   _____

Fires can't be made with dead embers, nor can enthusiasm be stirred by spiritless men. Enthusiasm in our daily work lightens effort and turns even labor into pleasant tasks.

James Mark Baldwin

. . . and Disappointment

*H*ow do you respond to disappointment? When Edgar sent off to the mail-order house and ordered a book on photography, he waited for the mailman to come every day. Finally, the mailman did come with a package. When Edgar opened that package he was terribly disappointed, even angry, because they had sent him a book on ventriloquism. He was really upset about it!

Edgar immediately started to package the book up and send it back, but on second thought he decided that as long as he had it he might as well see what he could do with it. You probably have guessed by now that Edgar's last name was Bergen. This was the renowned, world-famous ventriloquist who gave us Charlie McCarthy and Mortimer Snerd. He brightened days for a lot of people through his good, clean, wholesome humor, and in the process, Edgar Bergen became enormously successful.

Edgar Bergen took a simple thought, a simple idea—he took a lemon and made lemonade out of it. If you will look for the good, good will come from any and all situations!

Action Steps

1. Today I will take the first disappointment that comes my way and use it as an opportunity to turn a lemon into lemonade.
2. Today I will_____

_____

How you think when you lose determines how long it will be until you win.
David Schwartz

. . . and Elevators

We were touring the East and we came to Washington, D.C. Naturally, we wanted to see the Washington Monument, but as we approached we heard the guide loudly announcing that there would be a two-hour wait to ride the elevator to the top of the monument. However, with a smile on his face he then said, "There is no waiting to go to the top if you are willing to take the stairs."

And how true that is! It applies not only to the trip to the top of the Washington Monument, but of infinitely more importance, the trip to the top in the game of life. To speak accurately, though, the elevator to success is not only crowded, it is permanently out of order; there is no free ride. Every person on the climb upwards has to take the stairs. If you're willing to take those stairs, and take them one at a time, then I really can truthfully say to you, "I'll see *you* at the top!"

Action Steps

1. Today I will remember that there is no "free lunch," and remind myself that if I am going to get to the top, it will be due to my hard work.
2. Today I will_____

_____

You cannot help men permanently by doing for them the things they could and should do for themselves.

Edward Everett Hale

. . . and Getting Fired

Several years ago, my family and I were having dinner at one of the nicer restaurants in Dallas and the busboy came by to pour our water. "Pour" is the wrong word. He was really sloshing the water! It was obvious he was unhappy, so I commented, "You don't like your job, do you?" The boy belligerently replied, "No, I don't!" I said, "Well, don't worry about it because you're not going to have it very long."

Somewhat startled, he asked what I meant, so I went on to explain that, with his attitude, this restaurant could not afford to have him around, even if *he* paid *them*! Fortunately, the young man did a reverse. He really turned his attitude around.

Attitude is very important, regardless of what you do. Get your attitude right and you will perform better. If you perform better you become more valuable to yourself and to your employer. That's the way to keep your job *and* get a raise.

Action Steps

1. Today I will do more than I am paid to do, because I know that if I do more than I am paid to do, then I will be paid more for what I do.
2. Today I will_____
   _____

Work is man's greatest function. He is nothing, he can do nothing, achieve nothing, fulfill nothing without working.

J. M. Cowan

... and the Six-Figure Income

My good friend Wilbert Eichenberger, the executive director of the Institute for Successful Church Leadership, quotes Howard Kreshner in talking about the free marketplace. Mr. Kreshner points out that the incomes of the top sixty men at General Motors amounts to $2.30 for each car and truck the company makes. This is a very small price to pay for the expertise, judgment, and energy of these executives.

I use this example because, when the average person reads about the six- and occasionally seven-figure incomes of some top executives, they grow resentful and feel that that is the reason consumer items like automobiles are so expensive. However, when you break down the cost of their skill to the $2.30 per car amount, it really is a small price to pay.

Of course, there is always the chance that some of these men are selfish, but to satisfy their own desires they must confer vast benefits upon the public. As I have repeatedly said, you can get everything you want in life if you will just help enough other people get what they want. That's why the free market is so exciting—and it's also why it has produced for us the highest standard of living known to man.

Action Steps

1. Today I will recognize that I will be rewarded in direct proportion to my efforts, and therefore I will make the best effort I possibly can.
2. Today I will_____

_____

The best prize life offers is the chance to work hard at work worth doing.
Theodore Roosevelt

. . . and Your Language

*R*ecently I talked with an executive of a major company. We were discussing the possibility of his company using a certain professional speaker at their national sales meeting. They had listened to a recording of one of his talks. It was an excellent recording, but he used a couple of suggestive stories.

The executive told the speaker they could not use him because of these stories. The speaker assured him that for his group he would delete the stories. To this the executive replied, "No, we are really looking for a speaker who will not have to take such stories out for our benefit. We want a speaker who never had the stories in his talk in the first place."

Unusual? Not at all. I've never heard of anybody hiring a person because he "cussed" so convincingly, or knew a lot of dirty jokes. I doubt that any young girl has ever gone home and told her daddy that he just had to meet this cute boy who just moved to town, because he told the most suggestive stories she had ever heard! I do know of many jobs or promotions—and many romances—that were missed because of profanity or obscene language.

People who succeed and go to the top are those who realize the importance of keeping it *clean*. If you will keep it clean, your chances for success will be greatly enhanced.

Action Steps

1. Today I will be more aware than ever of my language and the impact it has on those around me.
2. Today I will_____

_____

Goodness is the only investment that never fails.

Henry David Thoreau

. . . Winning vs. Losing

My good friend, the outstanding platform speaker Denis Waitley, explains that the winning field goal kicker lines up for the field goal and says to himself, "If I kick this field goal it will put us in the Super Bowl and will be worth thirty thousand dollars to every man." The loser lines up and says, "If I miss this field goal, it will cost all my teammates thirty thousand dollars." That's the difference. According to Dr. Waitley, the winners concentrate on what they want to get; the losers concentrate on what they don't want—and they get it.

Undoubtedly the most destructive force in our lives is the negative use of our imaginations. Most people visualize the things they don't want, whether headache, bad cold, missed sale, or even inability to find a parking space. Losers think in terms of lack or loss; winners, according to Dr. Waitley, think of success and winning.

As the old saw goes, "Whether you think you can or think you can't, you are right!"

Action Steps

1. Today I will practice thinking like a winner by concentrating on what I want and thinking of success and winning.
2. Today I will_____

_____

He who fears being conquered is sure of defeat.

Napoleon Bonaparte

Choosing . . .

"He who chooses the beginning of a road, also chooses its outcome."

. . . Moods

*D*epression has been described as the harmful art of doing nothing. Depression is the feeling that life is hopeless and that there is no remedy, that nothing really matters. All of us have faced times when we didn't feel positive about our future. You know what I'm talking about—when you can't see your way out of a rough spot, and instead of sunshine you see only dark clouds.

Did you know that *you* control your moods? Your actions dictate your feelings, so with that in mind think about these three tips.

First, remember that all depression has anger as its root cause and that in virtually every case that anger is directed at an individual. Search your memory bank; if you are angry or bitter towards one or more people, go to them, tell them you forgive them, and ask them to forgive you.

Second, put some order in your life. In most cases depression is fed by loose ends in our lives. Get out your "do list" and get organized. Each task you complete will make you feel better.

Third, try to help someone. Dr. Karl Menninger of the Menninger Clinic in Topeka, Kansas, says that if you feel a nervous breakdown coming on you should seek someone who has a problem and help solve *that* problem. When you do, your own problem will often be solved. It's true: you can get everything you want in life if you will just help enough other people get what they want.

Action Steps

1. Today I will help someone "secretly"—I will do a kind thing for someone anonymously.
2. Today I will do something nice for _____ .
   (name)
3. Today I will_____

_____

Happiness is a perfume you cannot pour on others without getting a few drops on yourself.

Ralph Waldo Emerson

. . . Control

*R*emember that you alone are "in charge of the chicken."

The governor of Massachusetts was running hard for a second term. He had campaigned all morning, missed lunch, and arrived late in the day at a church barbecue. As he held out his plate, the tired woman on the other side of the table put one piece of chicken on it.

"Excuse me," he said, "could I have another piece of chicken?"

"Sorry, only one piece to a customer," she replied.

"Don't you recognize me?" he persisted. "I'm Christian Herter, the *governor* of this state!"

"And I'm the lady in charge of the chicken," she responded. "Move along, Mister." Such extreme devotion to responsibility may be unwarranted, but such commitment is commendable.

What are you in charge of today? Whether it's serving chicken or a state, take charge! Do it, do it well, and do it right. Don't let anybody or anything cloud your vision of your duty. Most importantly, always remember that even though you might not be "in charge of the chicken," you can and should be in charge of your life—and in control of your future.

Action Steps

1. Today I will take charge of my life, realizing that I control my future.
2. Today I will_____

No man can climb out beyond the limitations of his own character.
                                                                Robespierre

64

. . . to Take Action

Some people win in spite of the odds—and that select group can include you.

Angie Pikshus had every reason to decide life had dealt her an unfair hand. Her mother died when she was still a baby. She never really knew her father or the peaceful security of a stable home; instead she was moved from foster home to foster home. When she was in the eighth grade, she was moved to Arkansas to live with some relatives. Angie was an orphan, was twenty pounds overweight (and therefore was growing out of all of her clothes), and now, to top it off, she was moving away from her friends.

From time to time all of us have reason to believe that life has stacked the deck against us. At this point in her life, Angie Pikshus had ample reason to feel cheated, but she decided *to do something* about her situation. She decided she needed to lose weight, so she began running strictly for the exercise, to burn off that excess weight. The more she ran, the more she enjoyed and applied herself to the task. She continued to train and began entering races.

Angie, now a senior at Arkansas State University, has won three marathons and several ten-kilometer races. She has won the New Orleans Mardi Gras Marathon twice, the Memphis Express Marathon, and the Atlanta Avon 10-K, among other events.

Angie Pikshus had every reason to decide that life had declared her a loser, but she didn't. She excelled in spite of the obstacles. The exciting thing about this story is that the same principles of commitment, dedication, and *hard work* that helped her lose the weight and become a winning runner will also make her a winner in other areas of life.

P.S.: The same principles will work for you, too.

Action Steps

1. Today I will make a commitment to work as hard as necessary to reach my goals.
2. Today I will_____

_____

Complete success is not purchased at any one time, but rather on the install-ment plan.

Fraternal Monitor

. . . High Ideals

I'd like to encourage you to do some daydreaming and set your sights on higher objectives in your life.

A professor of economics gave a test to his class with three categories of questions. He instructed the students to choose one question from each section on the test. The first category was the hardest and worth fifty points. The second, which was not as hard, was worth forty points. The third, the easiest, was worth only thirty points.

When the papers were returned, the students who had chosen the hardest questions, the fifty-pointers, were given *A*s. The students who had chosen the forty-point questions received *B*s. Those students who had attempted to answer the thirty-point questions, the easiest ones, were given *C*s.

The students didn't understand, so they asked the professor how he graded the exam. The professor leaned back, smiled, and explained, "I wasn't testing your knowledge, *I was testing your aim.*"

Langston Hughes wrote, "Hold fast to dreams, for if dreams die, then life is like a broken-winged bird that cannot fly." Browning said, "A man's reach should exceed his grasp or what's a Heaven for?" One good thing about aiming for the moon is that you are not likely to come up with a handful of mud. Dream big, aim high, go for the fifty-point questions.

Action Steps

1. Today I will go for the fifty-point questions in my life.
2. Today I will_____

_____

The explanation of triumph is all in the first syllable.

. . . Positive Responses

*Y*our "blow-up" point has a lot to do with your "go-up" point. Recently in a restaurant I watched a man and his wife eat an absolutely miserable dinner. They had a terrible time because of an insignificant lapse of memory on the part of the waitress and a short fuse on the man's temper.

The man asked for a refill on his coffee and the waitress promised to get it right away.

On her way to the coffee pot, another customer asked for his check, explaining that he had a plane to catch. The waitress paused and then took care of his bill, in the process forgetting the earlier request for coffee. About three minutes later, the man who had requested the refill hit the ceiling. The evening went downhill from there.

It's a shame that so many times we let something of such minor consequence as this destroy an evening or ruin an event for ourselves and others. Realistically, situations like this often affect many phases of our lives, from family solidarity to business success. It has been said that our size is measured by what it takes to irritate us, so my question is, "What is your 'blow-up' point?" Restrain the "blow-up" and enhance your "go-up"!

Action Steps

1. Today I will pause before responding in *every* situation so that I will remain in control of myself and my destiny.
2. Today I will_____

_____

Whether on the road or in an argument, when you see red, stop!

. . . Character

Chris Schenkel has been callled the "good guy of sports" since 1952. According to Schenkel, it's no act. Despite criticism for being too praiseworthy and nonjudgmental in his broadcasting style, Schenkel replies, *"What I do is who I am.* If I had to go back, I wouldn't change one bit. I had some pressure put on me (to be more critical), but I got this far being what I am and I wouldn't change."

Chris Schenkel began his dream to be a broadcaster in the 1930s. He listened to baseball games on the radio and tried to copy the broadcaster's style. His father purchased an early audio disc recorder for Chris. Chris would record the games and practice mimicking the announcer. As a freshman at Purdue University, Schenkel took a summer job for WLBC in Muncie, Indiana, for eighteen dollars a week. He wrote commercials, collected payments from customers, and announced for twelve-hour shifts. In 1952 he began substitute announcing the ABC fights on radio and then began substitute announcing the New York Giants football games in the early days of television.

For many years Chris Schenkel paid his dues; today he's one of the most respected broadcasters in America. He did it with praise, not with criticism. Don't be afraid to let your principles show, but stand up for what you believe is right. As Chris Schenkel says, *what you do is who you are.*

Action Steps

1. Today I will remember that "what I do is who I am," and I will act accordingly.
2. Today I will_____

_____

Character is simply habit long continued.

. . . Selflessness

I'm told there is a tree in Indonesia called the "upas." This tree secretes poison and grows so full and thick that it kills all vegetation growing beneath it. It shelters, shades, and destroys. I'm sorry to say that I know some people like that—and I think you do, too.

They are self-centered and dominating. They take all the credit and try to keep the attention to themselves. They have no interest in helping others, but plenty of interest in using others. Like the upas tree, they provide no chance for anyone around them to blossom and mature and grow.

On the other hand, I can remember as a boy trying to balance on a railroad track. I couldn't walk too far without losing my balance. But if my buddy got on the other side, we could hold each other's hands and serve as balances for one another. We literally could have walked around the world.

You and I have a choice to make. We can choose to be like the upas tree—to put out selfish poisons, thinking only of ourselves and what we want and basking in our egos—or we can stretch out our hands to help others as we go through life. Disraeli said, "Life is too short to be little." It's true. You can use your life in service to others or waste it in very misguided selfishness. You can use people or make friends.

Action Steps

1. Today I will reach out to those I care about with a helping hand.
2. Today I will_____

_____

Kindness is one thing you can't give away—it always comes back.

. . . Problems

*E*ven if it involves something as simple as opening the ketchup bottle, you more than likely will deal today with a problem—which I more realistically define as an opportunity. Handling and solving those opportunities is a normal part of living life. We encounter them from every conceivable angle, from the time we get up in the morning until we go to bed at night.

Mature and successful living comes when we learn to handle these opportunities as quickly and with as little fanfare as possible. The sharp business executive moves papers across his desk at a remarkable clip, making quick and final decisions with years of experience behind each decision. The homemaker with three small children at home handles a number and incredible variety of opportunities each hour with the same expertise.

Opportunity-solving becomes a very important part of our make-up as we grow into maturity. Actually, our value to our employers and to ourselves is in direct proportion to the number and size of the so-called problems we solve each day. So when opportunities arise, be thankful and take the time to define them correctly. Learn the skill of quick analysis, and remember, if it weren't for "problems" in your business, your position might not be necessary in the first place. Ironing out the wrinkles is what most jobs are all about.

Action Steps

1. Today I will look at my problems as opportunities and realize that I can increase my value by being a problem-solver.
2. Today I will_____

_____

The doors of opportunity are marked "push" and "pull."

. . . Happiness

I believe a person needs to enjoy life. No matter how busy you are, you still have time to be one of two things: happy or unhappy. When you got up this morning, you might not have realized it, but you chose to be happy or unhappy.

Carol Burnett recently received a collection of poems from some children. One girl named Patricia wrote, "Happiness is to snuggle up in bed under all the blankets on a cold night. Happiness is just being happy." Happiness is just being happy.

June Callwood relates that historian Will Durant looked for happiness in knowledge and found disillusionment. He then sought happiness in travel and found weariness; in wealth and found discord and worry. He looked for happiness in his writing and was only fatigued. One day he saw a woman waiting in a car with a sleeping child in her arms. A man descended from a train and came over and gently kissed the woman and then the baby, very softly so as not to awaken him. The family drove away, leaving Durant with the stunning realization that *every normal function of life holds some delight*.

In your search for happiness and success, don't overlook your own backyard. And don't forget that happiness is like a kiss. In order to get any good out of it, you have to give it to someone else!

Action Steps

1. Today I will give away happiness and in so doing enjoy the rewards that follow.
2. Today I will_____

_____

The foolish man seeks happiness in the distance; the wise man grows it under his feet.

James Oppenheim

. . . Television

*W*hen someone asks the question, "Want a television job?," visions of glamor, recognition, fame, and fortune probably pop into your mind. What I'm going to share today will meet most of those criteria, but perhaps not in the way you'd expect.

The television job I have in mind for you as a parent or friend of a child is one of involvement. If parents get involved with what their kids see on T.V., then some T.V. can be good. Unfortunately, much of what you—or a kid—can see on the tube is anything but good. As an example think of this: an average of every seven and one-half minutes of prime-time viewing, drinking alcohol is presented as a fact of life, in a generally favorable light. This does not include the beer and wine commercials, the most persuasive advertisements on T.V.

The potential benefit of television—like a lot of things—hinges on parental involvement. So the job I have for you is not in front of the camera, but in a management position in front of the set. If you do your job well, you'll be successful where it counts the most—in your own home, with your own children and their friends. With this approach, chances are good you will hear your own children saying, "My folks are the greatest! They wanted the best for me and were willing to get involved to see that I got it!" What a payoff for your television job!

Action Steps

1. Today I will take control of my life *and* my television set. I will "manage" the input into the minds of myself and my family.
2. Today I will_____

_____

My objection to television is not merely that the quality of programs is depressingly low; it is also that the screen exercises a hypnotic effect on the majority of watchers. . . . It is a terrible slavery of the mind—and, as Aristotle warned us a long time ago, "The worst thing about slavery is that eventually the slaves get to like it."

Sidney J. Harris

. . . and Opportunity

Since I was raised in a small, Southern town during the Depression, I was exposed to a way of life that seems almost prehistoric by today's standards.

In the grocery store where I worked we sold molasses by the gallon, and dispensed it from a huge wooden barrel. In those days, money for candy and sweets was virtually nonexistent. A small boy with a sweet tooth and a serious fondness for molasses frequently came into the store. He would always make a beeline to that big barrel, take the top off, run his finger through the molasses, and lick it. That was his candy. The boss repeatedly warned him not to do it.

One day when the boss literally caught the boy in the act, in complete exasperation he lifted the little fellow up and dropped him into the barrel. As the little guy was sinking slowly out of sight, he could be heard to pray, "Oh, Lord, give me the tongue to equal this opportunity!"

When I write or speak I pray that God will give me the tongue (pen) to equal the opportunity. The molasses story is obviously a joke, but it's no joke when I say to you that opportunity frequently comes the way of those who unfortunately are unprepared to meet it. My advice and belief is that if you get ready for opportunity, opportunity always will be ready for you.

Action Steps

1. Today I will *prepare* for the opportunities that are sure to come my way.
2. Today I will_____

_____

Opportunities multiply as they are seized; they die when neglected.

74

. . . Communication

*W*hile Henry David Thoreau was living at Walden Pond, he saw some workmen stringing wires along the Fitchburg Railroad right-of-way. When he asked what they were doing, they proudly replied that they were stringing telegraph lines that would enable the people of Maine to talk to the people of Texas.

Despite the fact that this was the most sophisticated form of communication at that time, Thoreau was unimpressed with the newfangled invention. He asked, "But what if the people of Maine have nothing to say to the people of Texas, and the people of Texas have nothing to say to the people of Maine?"

If Thoreau were alive today, he would see communications systems far superior to the telegraph, but would he be impressed? Perhaps—but he might also raise the same question for us. The question is this: do you place more emphasis on your methods than your messages? Some people have something to say while others just have to say *something*. Which kind of person are you?

Action Steps

1. Today I will remember the important instructions that should come with each person's vocal ability: "Engage brain before operating mouth."
2. Today I will_____

_____

When you talk you only say something that you already know—when you listen you learn what someone else knows.

. . . to Follow Through

Ninety-five-year-old Helen Hill describes her high school days as wonderful, even if she never received her diploma. She and her five classmates received no formal diplomas, because the school they graduated from was in debt. But I'm happy to tell you that Helen Hill finally received that diploma. In May, 1983, Mrs. Hill, who is the oldest resident of South Thomaston, Maine, and the only surviving member of the class of 1907, received her diploma—seventy-six years late!

It's never too late to dream, to learn, or to change. Carl Carson decided to make a career change at the tender age of sixty-four. He moved from a successful car and truck leasing business to the consultation business. His goal was to sell his services to ten clients. Carl Carson reached that goal in March, 1983. He now puts out a monthly newspaper advising *twelve hundred* paying subscribers. He averages crisscrossing the nation *one hundred times a year* to speak at conventions and seminars. Carl Carson is seventy-five years old.

It's never too late to dream, to learn, or to change. People can always come up with excuses—like they're too old, or too young, or not the right color or sex. Life's not easy but it can be rewarding. You can't stop the calendar, but you can stop negative thinking and start using your unique abilities.

Action Steps

1. Today I will concentrate on what I can do instead of dwelling on what I cannot do.
2. Today I will_____

Experience shows that success is due less to ability than to zeal. The winner is he who gives himself to his work, body and soul.

Charles Buxton

. . . Determination

A young radio announcer, on the verge of success, was suddenly fired from his job. He was heartbroken, but when he got home he enthusiastically announced to his wife, "Honey, I've got a chance to go out on my own."

As so often happens, the event in life that seemed to be the most disappointing had the potential of being his biggest break. That young radio announcer took a very positive approach and did go out on his own. He created a program that later became known on T.V. as "People Are Funny." You probably watched the young broadcaster who became the number-one television personality for many years during the fifties and sixties—Mr. Art Linkletter.

Art has written a new book entitled *Yes, You Can!* in which he points out how one of the biggest disappointments in his early career turned out to be the springboard into his later success. The same principle can be applied to most of our lives. Failure and rejection seem to make us or break us. For the truly determined person, failure often provides the source of determination that is needed for that push over the top.

Be like Art Linkletter. Turn disappointment into determination and it will help take you to the top.

Action Steps

1. Today I will turn minor disappointments into major achievements by looking for the good in *everything* that comes my way.
2. Today I will_____

_____

Big shots are only little shots who keep shooting.

Christopher Morley

. . . Optimism

*W*inston Churchill often said, "I am an optimist—it doesn't seem to do much good being anything else." I think most of us would agree that a philosophy of optimism and forward-looking enthusiasm is a far better way of life than pessimism. We have learned over the course of time that we're happier and function better when we look with hope and excitement into the future.

But what many of us haven't learned is that our optimistic outlook is a result of a choice we have made. We choose our basic attitudes about life. That's why the statement by Winston Churchill means so much to me. I, too, am an optimist because I choose to be one. Pessimism and despair is not the way I choose to travel.

My choice is not made without reason. I most certainly have my reasons for choosing to live with enthusiasm and hope. It's my belief that the very creative center of all nature and all life is positive, optimistic, and hopeful. The choice is not blind, but a choice of reason and purpose. Based on the lives of the many winners I personally know, I truly believe you have many reasons to expect victory in your life.

Action Steps

1. Today I will use my God-given gift of choice to choose happiness over sadness, optimism over pessimism, and victory over defeat!
2. Today I will_____

_____

All the Declaration of Independence proclaims is the right to pursue happiness; you have to catch up with it yourself.

. . . to Fail

*T*he road to success is filled with people who fail. Sounds like a contradiction, doesn't it? Yes, it's very true. The road to success is filled with failures. "How could that be?" you ask. It is very simple: people who eventually become successful are those who are not afraid to try. They are people who know that failure is always a possibility in any endeavor. They don't like failure, they even abhor failure, but at the same time they are not afraid of it.

Did you know the greatest slugger of all time is also the man who for many years held the major league strikeout record? That's right, Babe Ruth, the legend himself, struck out more times than any other man who ever played the game of baseball until Mickey Mantle broke his strike-out record. Babe Ruth was not afraid to go to bat and take a healthy cut.

Interesting, isn't it? And it gives us an insight into what we mean when we make the strange statement that the road to success is filled with failures. These people are not permanent failures, that's for sure, but innovators, experimenters, challengers: people who realize they must pick themselves up and try again every time they fall. They know that as long as they get up one time more than they fall that they haven't failed. Here's hoping you are willing to go to bat, face the odds, and take your very best swing.

Action Steps

1. Today I will convert failure into achievement by reminding myself that every failure moves me one step closer to victory.
2. Today I will_____

_____

Many a man never fails because he never tries.

Norman MacEwan

. . . Friendly People

*D*on't judge a city by one nasty citizen or a person by one unpleasant experience. Here's why.

A young couple from New York came to Dallas. Unfortunately, the first man they met was apparently a direct descendant of the cruise director for the Titanic. The couple jumped to the erroneous conclusion that all Texans were that way. They complained that Texans were the most unfriendly people they had met. They griped that they had been in Texas for months and had met no new friends. Sadly enough their negative attitude eliminated any possibility of making friends.

Fortunately, all that changed one evening when a young man and his wife decided to take the couple around the town and let them see the "real" Dallas. They introduced them with enthusiasm to some neighbors and took them to church, as well as some sporting and social events. The new couple saw Dallas and Texans in their true light. Today the new couple are old friends to their many Texas neighbors. Today they out-brag most "native" Texans (those who have been here ten years).

The old adage, "Don't judge a book by its cover," is true when we refer to making first judgments about anything—people, cities, businesses, schools, or whatever. The message is clear. Don't jump to conclusions and hang a label on a person or town because of one unfortunate experience. Give them a second chance and both of you will be better off.

Action Steps

1. Today I will remove labels I have placed on _____
   (name)
   _____ and _____ and find out what
   (name)
   kind of people they really are.
2. Today I will_____
   _____

We cannot always oblige, but we can always speak obligingly.

Voltaire

. . . to Build

*T*he book *What's in a Name?*, published by Ark Books of Minneapolis, Minnesota, is an unusual and intriguing book. It lists about seven hundred first names and gives their literal meanings, character qualities, corresponding Scripture verses, and further explanations.

In the introduction to the book a story is told about a boy named Clayton who was called "Clay" by his friends. Clay's uncle started him on the wrong foot by equating clay with dirt. Clay had self-image and attitude problems throughout his life, until by chance he met John Hartzell, one of the book's three compilers. John explained to Clay that clay is not just dirt, but is an important substance, a raw material that when placed in the potter's hands becomes a thing of beauty and usefulness. He was told that God compared his own special people to clay. Clayton then realized his own self-worth, understood his uniqueness, and became a new man with a new outlook and a new direction.

Clay's story is sad, revealing, and exciting. It is sad that a thoughtless uncle brought unhappiness to a nephew he probably loved. It is revealing because it shows the importance of getting the correct information. The excitement of the story comes because it shows all of us that we can change our position in life by changing our thinking.

Action Steps

1. Today I will be aware of the power my words have and will use them positively.
2. Today I will_____

_____

Some of mankind's most terrible misdeeds have been committed under the spell of certain magic words or phrases.

James Bryant Conant

. . . Virtue

After the death of Freddie Prinze, one of the superstars of entertainment, Hollywood columnist Rona Barrett was asked a question. "Do you know of any other superstars in the world of entertainment, music, or athletics who might also be in danger of either deliberately or accidentally taking their own lives?" Rona responded, "I don't know of even one superstar who is *not* in danger of either deliberately or accidentally taking his or her own life, because I don't know a single one who is really happy."

That's sad, isn't it? On the surface these people seem to have everything: youth, health, money, fame, and so much charisma they have to hire bodyguards to protect them from members of the opposite sex. But with all of this, they are unhappy. The reason is simple. What you *have* won't make you happy; it's what you *are* that counts.

Parents, I encourage you to not spend money giving your children "things." Give them yourself, your time, and your unconditional love. Teach them the old-fashioned virtues of honesty, character, integrity, faith, love, loyalty, and dependability. With these ingredients your children can manufacture their own happiness.

Action Steps

1. Today I will spend quality *and* quantity time with those I love.
2. Today I will remember to teach the "old-fashioned virtues" through my positive example.
3. Today I will_____

_____

He who is virtuous is wise; and he who is wise is good; and he who is good is happy.

. . . Retreat

Gene Tunney, the former heavyweight champion of the world, trained for his fights with Jack Dempsey by running backwards. Tunney was not afraid of Dempsey, but he regarded Dempsey as a devastating puncher. He knew that if he was hit by Dempsey he might be seriously hurt, and that a hurt fighter instinctively goes on the attack and generally gets knocked out.

To guard against the possibility of instinctively making the wrong move, Tunney trained for his fight by running backwards many miles. His strategy paid off in the famous fight of the long count. When Tunney got up after the long count, he backed away from Dempsey and fought a delaying action until the end of the round. In the next round, having completely regained his strength and senses, Tunney knocked Dempsey down and went on to win the fight.

Tunney won because he prepared in advance. In life, each one of us is going to encounter difficulties. Since we can't tailor-make our situations, we should tailor-make our attitude in advance to deal with negative situations and negative people. That's the way to win in the opportunities that life offers us every day.

Action Steps

1. Today I will prepare mentally for all opportunities by *visualizing* my key activities in advance. Two important activities that I want to mentally rehearse *before* encountering are a) _____ _____ and b) _____.
2. Today I will_____
_____

What we see depends mainly on what we look for.

John Lubbock

. . . in America

*P*eter Jenkins walked 4,751 miles and wore out about thirty-five pairs of shoes in a five-year trek across America. He did it because he wanted to give America another chance. Information he had picked up in college and by reading the "state of the state" had made him literally sick of his country. In short, he had a case of "stinkin' thinkin'" that was fast turning into a case of "hardening of the attitudes." The trip worked, because after traveling all over this land and getting to know America and Americans, he became totally excited about and completely dedicated to America.

Obviously, most of us can't take five-year trips walking around the country, but by listening to positive comments, reading good books and magazines, and taking an optimistic view of good things that are happening in America, I believe you, too, will be just as sold on America as is Peter Jenkins. When this happens you will recognize the beauty and the tremendous possibilities America offers you. As a result, your zest and enthusiasm for life will be rekindled, which means I will see *you* at the top!

Action Steps

1. Today I will read at least one positive article (magazine or newspaper) about our great land.
2. Today I will share at least one positive comment about our country. I will start with _____ .
3. Today I will_____

_____

Those who would increase the love they have for our native country need only reside for some time in a foreign one.

84

... the Future

An interesting question is whether opportunity lies in the person or in the job. The answer is perhaps that it lies in both. I personally know people in the taxicab business who are doing well, while many are just eking out an existence. I know people owning service stations who are doing well, but there are others who are going broke.

Rather than dwelling on many examples, though, let's take a case in point. I've often wondered—especially at hotels and airports—how a cab driver could sit in his cab from five minutes to as long as three hours waiting on a fare, doing nothing but smoking, listening to the radio, or walking around in complete boredom. During the time he is waiting he could acquire a magnificent education that could qualify him for a hundred and one different—and in most cases, better—jobs. He could become an expert in computer science, or even acquire the basic knowledge for an education in law.

Just fifteen minutes a day enables the average reader to complete fifteen books each year. The point is simple: regardless of what you do, use your spare time to really get ahead in life.

Action Steps

1. Today I will effectively use *all* my time by having a plan for my spare time.
2. Today I will_____

_____

The past is present in the future.

Dr. Louis L. Mann

. . . Discomfort

Many years ago, heavyweight champion "Gentleman Jim" Corbett was doing his roadwork when he saw a fisherman pulling in one fish after another. But Corbett noticed that the fisherman threw the big ones back and kept the small ones. Curiosity got the better of Gentleman Jim, so he asked the fisherman why he kept the little ones and threw the big ones back. The fisherman responded, "Man, I really hate to do it, but I don't have any choice. All I've got is a small frying pan!"

Now before you laugh, let me remind you that he is really talking about you and me. Many times when we get a big idea we are inclined to say, "Oh, no, Lord, not such a big one! All I've got is a small frying pan!" We even elaborate by saying, "Besides, Lord, if it is such a good idea someone else would already have thought about it. Just give me a little one, Lord. Don't take me out of my comfort zone; don't make me sweat and stretch and use my ability."

The message of the story is when you get a big idea, get busy on it. The same God who gave you the big idea in the first place will give you the little pieces to make that big dream a reality.

Action Steps

1. Today I will enlarge my "frying pan" and step out of my comfort zone. I will accomplish this by taking the following steps:
   a) _____ b) _____
   c) _____

2. Today I will _____

_____

Little pots soon boil over.

86

. . . Change

*W*ould you believe a four-bedroom house could be built today for less than a thousand dollars?

John Olberding of Newkirk, Oklahoma, has beaten the high cost of building a new home in a very interesting way. John worked for several years at the Cowley County Landfill Area and was appalled at the amount of waste. Perfectly good building materials, furniture, and appliances were being thrown away. He felt that these materials could be saved and put to good use.

He decided to start saving some of these waste materials, and before long he had enough lumber, steel siding, and plumbing fixtures to start his own house. He drew up the plans, poured the concrete, and with the help of a few friends, put up the walls.

He hasn't had to skimp on anything in the house. The walls are filled with insulation and the floors are carpeted throughout the four-bedroom house. The new dishes, silverware, refrigerator, and kitchen stove all came from the landfill in good working order.

John Olberding, a man of ingenuity, is living very comfortably in his two-story house, built for less than one thousand dollars. Looks like that old American do-it-yourself ingenuity is still alive and well. Yep, where there's a will—there's a way.

Action Steps

1. Today I will look for the hidden opportunities in my life.
2. Today I will_____

_____

Times of change are times of fearfulness and times of opportunity. Which they may be for you, depends upon your attitude toward them.

Ernest C. Wilson

. . . Profit

*W*hen I was a young boy I worked in a grocery store. One day nothing was going on; the boss was a little concerned that nobody was working. So he singled me out, pointed to a shelf, and suggested that I dust it off or clean it out. I rather indignantly replied, "Well, Mr. Anderson, there are only two cans of tomatoes."

Well, the way I said "only" wasn't exactly what the boss wanted to hear. He stopped me dead in my tracks and said, "Now let me tell you something about those two cans of tomatoes. They came in a full case of twenty-four. We've sold the first twenty-two. That means we've got our money back. Our profit is wrapped up in those last two cans of tomatoes, and it's out of profit that I'm going to pay you. Now what do you think of those two cans of tomatoes?" I looked at him, grinned, and said, "Mr. Anderson, they are beautiful!"

What we need to do is to do the best we can to help the boss make more profit. Then he can pay us more! If we do that, the boss wins and we will win as well.

Action Steps

1. Today I will remember that I can get everything in life I want if I will just help enough other people get what they want.
2. Today I will_____

> *Be interested in the "how" of your work, and the "how much" will take care of itself.*

. . . a Helping Hand

Surely one of the saddest creatures around is the one we call the "prisoner of hope." You undoubtedly have seen him. This is the person who hopes that someday a wealthy relative will die and leave him vast riches. The prisoner of hope hopes that someday, walking down the street, he will see a box, will kick the box, and will receive out of it thousands and thousands of dollars, enough to give him security—or so he thinks.

He's the kind of person that goes down to the seashore and looks out to see if his ship is coming in, when in reality he knows that it has never left the port. This is particularly sad because often he has ability—real ability.

The prisoner of hope hasn't discovered that if you really want to find a helping hand, you should look down at the end of your own sleeve—because that's where it's going to be! Now if you will use those hands at the ends of your own sleeves, you will find the answers to many of the problems that have been eluding you to this point in your life.

Action Steps

1. Today I will accept responsibility for my actions and will look for a helping hand only at the end of my own sleeve.
2. Today I will_____

_____

If I am not for myself, who will be? But, if I am only for myself, what am I?
Hillel

. . . Action

*A*re you the type of person who makes things happen, watches things happen, or doesn't even know what happened? These are the three kinds of people: the doers, the onlookers, and the uninterested.

The doers are those energetic people who are always willing to try a new approach or test a new product. They are involved in activities with their families and communities. They are genuinely interested in new ideas and in putting those ideas into action.

Then there are the onlookers. These are the people who are interested in new ideas, but are only interested in watching someone else go to the trouble of testing them. They want part of the action *after* the risk is removed—after they know everything is going to work out okay.

And finally, the third group is the uninterested. These are the people who are neither interested in testing new ideas, nor in watching anyone else do so. They want to coast through life; they never fully understand that the only way to coast is downhill.

Let me urge you today to develop the habit of action and exploration. Yes, it is a choice that is entirely up to you. We become *doers* by choosing to *do*!

Action Steps

1. Today I will begin to develop the habit of action by choosing to be a doer.
2. Today I will_____

He that is busy is tempted by but one devil; he that is idle, by a legion.
Thomas Fuller

. . . Your Mental Health

Many people leave the radio or television on, but say they "don't pay any attention to it." This is dangerous.

When you are concentrating on watching or listening, your conscious mind stands guard over your subconscious mind. It rejects the ridiculous claims, ideas, and statements that often come in over the airways. However, when you are *not* consciously listening (even while you are asleep), the subconscious mind is wide open and you are bombarded with some incredibly destructive concepts. The housewife who leaves the television on for the "noise" or "company," but whose mind is somewhere else, is equally being bombarded with absurd ideas.

So parents, when your children say they can study better with the television or radio on, let me urge you to turn it off. The external sound makes concentration difficult and leaves the mind open to a lot of garbage.

Action Steps

1. Today I will be a conscious participant in the programming of my mind.
2. Today I will_____

_____

A closed mind is an enigma, indeed. Nothing ever goes in—but odd things are forever coming out.

Lawrence Dunphy

. . . Good Habits

*I*n the game of life, most of us strive for the top and live and work in the hope that we will build successful lives. To accomplish this objective, we must understand that if we do not consciously form good habits, we will unconsciously form bad ones. Every person who has become successful has formed the habit of doing things he either dislikes doing or does not do very well.

Interestingly enough, many of the characteristics we acquire are simply the results of bad habits. Fear is a habit. So are self-pity, defeat, anxiety, despair, and hopelessness. Whining, griping, and complaining are all simply bad habits. Even being negative is a bad habit.

You can eliminate these bad habits with two simple resolutions (now I did not say it would be *easy*—I said it is simple). The resolutions are "I can" and "I will!" So make these two resolutions and you will become an even bigger winner in the game of life.

Action Steps

1. Today I will consciously form good habits by repeating to myself "I can" and "I will!"
2. Today I will_____

_____

Good resolutions are easier to break than bad habits.

. . . Friends

Your friends definitely influence you—either for the good or for the bad.

In Belleville, Illinois, at Belleville Township High School West, the 1979 winners of the Hy Life Citizenship Awards included four young people who came out of a group of eleven friends who, with just one exception, had been together since grade school. It is interesting to note that all eleven members of the group were in the finals before the eight winners were selected. That's about as strong a case as I have ever heard for associating with winners!

You do become part of what you are around, whether it's good, bad, or indifferent. In the last few years this has often been referred to as "peer-group pressure," in many cases associated with drug abuse and sexual promiscuity. It is exciting to know that peer-group pressure to excel is also alive and well. Want to be a winner? Associate with winners!

Action Steps

1. Today I will take the time to study my friends and evaluate whether I am influencing them or they are influencing me. I will also determine whether this influence is positive or negative.
2. Today I will_____

We are more than half what we are by imitation. The great point is to choose good models and to study them with care.

Lord Chesterfield

. . . the Challenge

When Winston Churchill retired for the second time from his post as prime minister of England, he was invited to address the graduating class at Oxford University. Sir Winston was seated at the head table, dressed in his formal wear—including his ever-present top hat, cane, and cigar.

After an extended and too-lengthy introduction, he walked to the podium. Grabbing the lectern in both hands, he paused for a number of seconds and looked at his audience. Then, in that Churchillian way that was uniquely his, he looked at them for a full thirty seconds and said, "Never, never, never give up!" Then another long pause, and with even greater emphasis and eloquence, he repeated, "Never, never, never give up!" He looked at the audience a few more seconds and sat down.

Undoubtedly, this presentation was the shortest major address in history. It also was one of Churchill's most memorable.

If you will take the advice of Winston Churchill, then I really will see you at the top!

Action Steps

1. Today I will "never, never, never give up!"
2. Today I will_____

> Don't get discouraged; it is often the last key in the bunch that opens the lock.

. . . What You Want

*A*re you guilty of asking for what you don't really want?

I know you personally wouldn't do this, but here's one instance. Have you ever seen someone come to work with a sniffle? You comment on the sniffle only to have the person respond, "Well, it just started this morning, but my colds don't get too bad until the third day, and then they really kill me." That person is asking for what he doesn't really want!

Think of the person who wakes up or comes to work with a slight headache. Somebody comments on it, and the person responds, "Well, it's slight right now, but it always is in the morning. It's not until about three o'clock in the afternoon that it really kills me!" The person is asking for what he doesn't want.

Do you ever look at your watch late at night as you lie down and say to yourself, "Boy, I bet I'm gonna be tired and am gonna feel bad tomorrow!"? If you have, then you've been guilty of asking for what *you* didn't want. What a shame that we use our imagination in such a negative way, when we could use it in a positive way and get the things we do want.

Why not try it the other way? Talk to yourself in a positive fashion, and you'll discover that it's nice to ask for—and often to get—the things you *do* want.

Action Steps

1. Today I will speak only positively to myself. I will ask for the things that I *do* want.
2. Today I will_____

_____

Optimism is the determination to see more in something than there is.

Courage

Courage may be taught, as a child is taught to speak.
Euripides

... to Overcome Defeat

*T*here's a silver lining in every cloud. Consider the clouds in this man's career:

He was a grade-school dropout.

He went bankrupt running a small country store and spent fifteen years paying off his debts.

He ran for office in the House of Representatives and was defeated twice.

He ran for office in the Senate and was defeated twice.

He was attacked daily by the press.

He was despised by half a nation.

He had several physical problems and was described as less than handsome.

During his term as president, his country went through its bloodiest period ever.

Even when he delivered a speech that became a classic, the audience either was indifferent or thought it was too short.

Despite the clouds, imagine how many people all over the world for over a hundred years have been inspired by this awkward, rumpled, and brooding man—Abraham Lincoln. Don't give up. Every cloud has its silver lining.

Abraham Lincoln was a great man who did great things. Throughout his experiences of defeat he was encouraged by many factors—perhaps mostly by the influence of his mother and stepmother. Will you give in, or will you listen for encouragement and overcome defeat?

Action Steps

1. Today I will make decisions based on long-range impact, not short-term gain.
2. Today I will *be aware* that my actions are influencing others, and I will accept this responsibility.

3. Today I will_____

_____

> *What is defeat? Nothing but education; nothing but the first step to something better.*
>
> Wendell Phillips

. . . over Ridicule

*T*o look at him today you would find it difficult to believe that in August, 1974, Clarence Gass awoke unable to breathe, thinking he had had *literally* breathed his last breath. However, the forty-one-year-old eventually regained his breath.

His health problem that August night was no mystery. He was going through three and a half packs of cigarettes and twenty-four cans of beer a day. He stopped weighing at the 265-pound mark when he had a forty-three-inch waist. That very morning, after his frightening experience, Clarence Gass got down on his knees and asked God to help him.

He quit drinking and smoking. He began to walk and then jog every night. Before the year was out, he was jogging four to five miles a day. Clarence went from more than 265 pounds to 150 pounds. His blood pressure dropped from 150 over 100 to 120 over 72. He has now run in ten marathons.

According to Gass, "It takes more courage than you can imagine for a fat person to get out and run in front of other people. It's a slow process and you must be patient. But it *is* possible. *You can do it.* Don't quit!"

Think about it: the odds are great that your physical condition is not as bad and your personal habits are not nearly as destructive as Clarence Gass's were in 1974. However, the odds are even greater that his physical condition and personal habits are both better than yours today. The question is this: If Clarence Gass can change to health and activity is there any real reason why you can't?

Action Steps

1. Today I will remember to ask for God's help in all my activities.
2. Today I will exercise in some fashion. It may be for five minutes or for one hour, but I will exercise today.
3. Today I will_____

Every day God makes silk purses out of sows' ears.

. . . over Despair

An automobile accident ten days before his high school graduation left Shane Vermoort classified as a quadriplegic. A friend was killed in the accident.

All of his life, Shane had wanted to be a doctor. But was it still possible for him as a quadriplegic—or was it really the impossible dream?

Shane went through a year of rehabilitation and then went to Southern Illinois University, where he received a B.A. in physiology. His goal was medical school, but he was rejected time and again by medical schools all over America.

Eventually, he was accepted at the Medical College of Georgia. He excelled in his preparation and received the Clinical Neuroscience Award, was elected president of the Medical Honor Society, and became the first student to graduate from the college in a wheelchair. Shane reflects, "People have a tendency to reflect on what we *don't* have. If people would just look in the mirror and focus on the *good* things, they would be a lot better off."

Shane is telling all of us not to look down in despair on what we don't have but to look up in hope and use what we do have. It certainly worked for him and I'm convinced it will work for you.

Action Steps

1. Today I will review my positive qualities and will be grateful for the talents and abilities I have.
2. Today I will_____

_____

Expect the best. Prepare for the worst. Take what comes.

. . . and Belief

*A*dmiral David Farragut, best remembered for his courage at Mobile Bay in 1864, listened as Admiral Samuel Dupont listed the reasons why he failed to get his fleet into Charleston Harbor and win the battle. When Dupont finished his explanation, Admiral Farragut replied, "There is one reason more. You did not *believe* you could."

Everyone knew that Glenn Cunningham would never walk again—everyone, that is, except for Glenn Cunningham and his mother. No one thought that he could ever win a footrace, except for Glenn Cunningham and his mother. His legs were badly burned in a schoolroom fire. But Glenn Cunningham walked, ran, and became the world's fastest miler. Glenn Cunningham believed in himself.

Sylvester Stallone was told by over fifty Hollywood producers that he had little ability as a writer. He was told he was wasting his time trying to market his script. But Sylvester Stallone believed in his ability, even though virtually every producer in Hollywood tried to convince him that there was no hope. The screenplay the producers turned down was *Rocky*. Sylvester Stallone believed in his ability.

Many people and obstacles might work to prevent you from reaching your goal, but you can overcome them. The most *devastating* obstacle is *your* own lack of belief. You can do anything you want to do if you believe and are willing to work. Shakespeare said, "Our doubts are traitors and make us lose the good we oft might win by fearing to attempt." Conrad Hilton remarked, "Man, with God's help and personal dedication, is capable of anything he can dream."

Action Steps

1. Today I will *not* be influenced by those "no" people who would place limitations on me.
2. Today I will _____

Be not afraid of life. Believe that life is worth living, and your belief will help create the fact.

. . . and Risk

*I*t's a simple truth—anything you do involves risk.
To drive a car is to risk having a wreck.
To apply for a job is to risk not being hired.
To try out for a play is to risk not getting the part.
To enter college is to risk flunking out.
To smile is to risk that no one will smile back.
To love is to risk rejection and hurt.
To speak is to risk that no one will listen.
To hope is to risk despair.
To dream is to risk appearing the fool.
To climb is to risk falling back down.

One ingredient I've noticed in the personality of almost every successful person I know is the the *courage to risk failure.* To try is definitely to risk failure, but what is your alternative? To do nothing, have nothing, and be nothing. When you do absolutely nothing you've avoided failure, but you also have avoided success. Anything of importance in life involves risk; if you don't try you can't do. Don't be afraid to reach for your dreams. As Will Rogers once said, "You've got to go out on a limb sometimes, because that's where the fruit is!"

Action Steps

1. Today I will risk by choosing one of the ten simple risks above. I choose to _____ .
2. Today I will_____

_____

The misfortunes hardest to bear are usually those which never happen.
James Russell Lowell

. . . and Security

*O*ften we have to make a choice between security and a touch of daring. Security is good sometimes, but a challenge also has its rewards.

Recently I saw a sailing vessel with sails hanging limp and lifeless on the mast. The vessel was not moving, but sat motionless and tranquil on the slick, calm surface of the harbor. The ship was safe and secure, but it wasn't going anywhere.

Human beings are like that. We can remain safe and secure in the harbor, living a life without daring and danger, or we can lift our sails and catch the wind, challenge the sea, give up certain security and tranquility, and take on the world. The person who faces the challenge and is willing to give up some security is the person moving from one place to the next. Until that sailing ship catches the breeze it will remain forever in the harbor.

We human beings are made to catch the wind in our sails and move out and explore our own timber. We are not created to be totally safe or totally stationary.

Remember that man and nature are 180 degrees apart in one respect. We use up nature's resources by using them up; we use up man's natural resources by not using them at all. This could be the reason Oliver Wendell Holmes pointed out that the greatest tragedy in America was the fact that most people go to their graves with their music still in them. I encourage you to unfurl those sails, catch the wind, use your ability, and let the music come out. I'll see you at the top!

Action Steps

1. Today I will use my natural resources and move out of the "comfort zone."
2. Today I will_____

_____

The superior man thinks always of virtue; the common man thinks of comfort.
Confucius

. . . and Appearance

I've used Phyllis Diller's example of success to inspire people in my book *See You at the Top,* and it was difficult for me to realize that she recently celebrated her sixty-fourth birthday. She said she celebrated with four cakes because one wouldn't hold all the candles. She quipped that she's doing something about that—she's now taking *birthday* control pills.

This remarkable standup comic has come a long way since collection people were knocking her door down while she was struggling to support three children. The seemingly carefree comedienne gives a peek at her inner feelings when she mentions her facelift and claims that she's prettier now than when she was born. (Bob Hope kids that she was so ugly at birth that the doctor slapped her mother!) Seriously, she says the facelift didn't affect her career but it did change her private life. "I feel better because when you look good it does your spirit good."

Telephone sales people who dress as if they were meeting people face to face outsell the casually dressed; teachers who wear a tie or dress are more effective than those who dress in open-neck shirts or slacks; students in dress clothes learn better than the T-shirt and blue-jean crowd; those who dress as if they care, usually do. You may not need a "facelift," but if you will do what you can to look good, it will make you feel good—and successful!

Action Steps

1. Today I will take special care with my personal appearance.
2. Today I will_____

> *Oh, would some power the gift to give us, to see ourselves as others see us.*
> Robert Burns

. . . and Integrity

I believe integrity is responding courageously in the face of adversity. Ryven Ezinga retired in 1972 from his one-man carpenter shop in Grand Rapids, Michigan. But he still stays busy using his power tools to create beautiful African violet stands in his small basement woodworking shop.

Now, it doesn't sound too unusual for a retired carpenter to still be involved in his lifelong trade, even if he is seventy-six years old. But two years ago, Ryven Ezinga became totally blind. Yet he's never let his lack of sight stop him from doing what he likes to do. Mr. Ezinga designs, builds, and finishes furniture in his basement workshop, using power tools including a table saw, lathe, router, sander, and sabre saw. He also recently invented a set of measuring devices in Braille, a creation that no doubt will help many others for years to come. All of these accomplishments are tributes to Ryven Ezinga, a man who didn't give up.

I love the real life story of Ryven Ezinga for at least two reasons. One is that this man who epitomizes positive thinking is the father of Zig Ziglar Corporation President Ron Ezinga. The second reason is that Ryven Ezinga is a man who lives with integrity. He has responded with creativity and courage in the face of adversity.

Action Steps

1. Today I will remember that if I respond courageously in the face of adversity, my opportunities will be multiplied.
2. Today I will_____

_____

All of us are always going to do better tomorrow, and we would, too, if only we started today.

. . . and Hardships

*T*here's a beautiful statue in Mexico that bears the unusual title, *In Spite Of.* The name was given to honor the sculptor rather than the subject in stone. It happened this way. During the time he was creating the statue, the sculptor suffered an accident and lost his right hand. But he was so determined to finish the statue that he learned how to chisel with his left hand. So the statue was entitled, *In Spite Of,* because in spite of his handicap, the sculptor completed his work.

In spite of blindness, Milton wrote. In spite of deafness, Beethoven composed. In spite of blindness and deafness, Helen Keller made speeches. In spite of rheumatic hands, Renoir painted. In spite of losing his right hand, the Mexican sculptor completed the statue with his left hand.

In spite of being blind, deaf, crippled, old, arthritic, poor, young, persecuted, or uneducated, people have overcome, excelled, accomplished, and triumphed. *And you can, too.* Reach for your goal in spite of your hardships and problems and I *will* see you at the top!

Action Steps

1. Today I will overcome _____ in spite of
   _____ .

2. Today I will _____
   _____

Character may be manifested in the great moments, but it is made in the small ones.

Phillips Brooks

. . . and Helping Others

*I*n 1977, *Guideposts* magazine reported the story of a man hiking in the mountains. He was taken by surprise by a sudden snowstorm and quickly lost his way. Since he was not dressed for the chilling temperature, he knew he needed to find shelter fast or he would freeze to death. Despite all of his efforts, time slipped by and his hands and feet became numb. He knew his time was short.

Then he literally tripped over another man who was almost frozen to death. The hiker had a decision to make: continue in hopes of saving himself or try to help this stranger in the snow.

In an instant he made his decision and threw off his wet gloves. He knelt beside the man and began massaging his arms and legs. The man began to respond and together they were able to find help.

The man was later informed that by helping another, he had *helped himself*. The numbness that had stricken him vanished while he was massaging the stranger's arms and legs. Every day of my life I become more convinced that the surest way to reach the summits of life is to help other people reach their plateaus.

Action Steps

1. Today I will help _____ , by
   (name)
   _____ , and by so doing, both of us will
   (service)
   benefit.
2. Today I will_____

_____

Live and let live is not enough; live and help live is not too much.

Orin E. Madison

. . . and Work

*Y*ou can go to the depths of despair and still come out on top. Carolyn Stradley is a beautiful example of this statement. She has been to the depths at least two times in her life: as a young mother of twenty-six, her husband died; and at thirty-two she was refused by three banks the capital to start her own business.

She didn't quit. She worked harder and eventually got the money from a credit company to start her own construction company. Yes, Carolyn Stradley is in the construction business, but her mind is certainly not like concrete—it is definitely not all mixed up and permanently set!

She expects to make fifty thousand dollars this year. She travels to other countries, scuba dives, sky dives, camps with her daughter, and still works twelve hours a day. She knows that even though she has an idea, a dream, the most practical, beautiful, workable philosophy in the world won't work—if *she* won't. Too many people quit looking for work as soon as they find a job. Carolyn Stradley isn't one of those. I'm betting you're not either.

Action Steps

1. Today I will realize that others can stop me temporarily, but that I am the only one who can stop myself permanently.
2. Today I will_____

_____

Why wish for the privilege of living your past life again? You begin a new one every morning.

Robert Quillen

108

. . . and Closed Doors

Most people have a dream of starting their own business. Eldon Kamp had been thinking about the possibilities for a long time when he was seriously injured in his work as a barge captain on the Mississippi River. He was afraid the accident would mean the end of his business. After months of painful surgery and convalescing, the future looked rather bleak.

But Eldon had always been handy with woodwork. He began to tinker a bit with cabinetmaking in his spare time. He carved some ornaments for the new home of a friend, and they were so skillfully done that he got another order, and then another. It wasn't long before Eldon had to hire a helper to keep up with the orders for handcarved wooden ornaments for new homes. Today Eldon has six fulltime workers in his cabinet and woodwork shop and has opened a new business that provides janitorial service for the buildings in his area.

Eldon Kamp's accident did end his career as a barge captain, but it launched him on what promises to be an even more successful career in an entirely different field. It often happens that when a door is closed, a window opens—but we have to look for that window.

Action Steps

1. Today I will look for the opportunities that always accompany adversity.
2. Today I will_____

Those who dare not, do not!

109

. . . and Adversity

*L*ife is what you make it. To put it another way, you can't change the cards life has dealt you, but you can determine the way you'll play them.

When Wendy Stoeker of Cedar Rapids, Iowa, was a freshman at the University of Florida, she placed third in the girls' state diving championship. She missed first by two and a half points. While swimming in the number two spot as only a freshman on the highly competitive Florida swim team, Wendy was carrying a full academic load.

Wendy sounds like a happy, positive coed, capable of making life whatever she wishes it to be, doesn't she? She is such a person. As a matter of fact, Wendy Stoeker already has made life what she wants it to be, even though she was born with no arms. Wendy has no arms, and yet she enjoys bowling, water skiing, and types at over forty-five words a minute. She is studying to be a physical therapist—and I'll lay you odds she will make it.

Let me encourage you to follow the example of Wendy Stoeker and think positively about what you want in life, regardless of the obstacles. Remember, life is what you make it.

Action Steps

1. Today I will concentrate on what I can do instead of what I cannot do.
2. Today I will_____

Success is never final and failure never fatal. It's courage that counts.

. . . and Inner Beauty

*T*here is at least one Miss America who believes that inner beauty is just as important as outer beauty. Donna Axum grew up in a small town in Arkansas and, like many girls in their adolescent years, she was very, very shy and unsure of her own place in life. Donna did not perceive herself as a beauty queen; as a matter of fact, she thought she was unattractive. But Donna had something that proved far more powerful than mere physical beauty—an inner charm and radiance, an inner glow that she believed could be brought to the surface.

She decided to try to bring her "inner beauty" out. After several months of physical exercise and effort learning the pageant skills of walking and standing, she entered a beauty contest. Donna lost that first contest, but that didn't discourage her. She entered another and another and, finally in 1963, after sixteen pageants, she became Miss Arkansas. And yes, she then became Miss America. That same inner glow, charm, and a considerable amount of hard work also has made her a successful platform speaker and T.V. personality, now with her own program.

The really good news, though, is that there is a presence, a glow, that is inside each and every one of us. Finding your own inner beauty and bringing it to the surface might not make you a Miss America, but it will make you a winner.

Action Steps

1. Today I will work to bring out my positive "inner qualities" so that I can be even more effective. Some of my best inner qualities are

   _____ , _____ ,

   and _____ .
2. Today I will_____

   _____

A man who has reformed himself has contributed his full share towards the reformation of his neighborhood.

Norman Douglas

. . . and Control

*H*e came to the professional football league in 1961. His scouting report was less than exciting, but he was the only one who didn't believe it.

That report said, "Too small for a quarterback, too slow on his feet and too weak—cannot take the punishment." After reading that scouting report by the experts you would probably get the idea that this young man should take a nice, safe job outside the rough and tumble world of professional football. How would you feel if you read that scouting report about yourself?

The young man from Georgia who was the subject of that report was a determined fellow. He not only made the team that first year, he became the first string quarterback in a very short time. He not only became first string, but he developed the reputation of being an excellent scrambler and thrower. As a matter of fact, Fran Tarkenton not only lasted longer in the NFL than any other quarterback, he passed for more yards than any quarterback in the history of the game. Yes, Fran Tarkenton of the Minnesota Vikings is one of the all-time leading passers in the National Football League.

Don't give up on yourself even if you get a bad scouting report. After all, you are the one who will determine what you will do with *your* ability.

Action Steps

1. Today I will take control of my future and make out my own scouting report.
2. Today I will_____

I have no economic radar to penetrate the future, but we can make it what we will it to be. Of that I am sure.

Bernard M. Baruch

. . . and Toughness

*B*rian Taylor is a nine-year-old boy who rode his bike over one hundred miles and raised one hundred dollars for the American Cancer Society. That feat would be enough in itself, but there is much more to the story, for Brian Taylor has only one leg.

That's right, it isn't easy for him to ride a bike. He had to beg his mother for the chance to learn. And she naturally was concerned after he had suffered a number of scrapes, cuts, and bruises and had torn up two brand new bicycles in the process. Brian's ride took some real effort and ingenuity.

Finally, Brian put a strap over the pedal of the bike to keep his foot fastened to it. Now he can ride like a pro. The proof of that is his hundred-mile ride in the bike-a-thon. Isn't it amazing what can be done when the desire is there! It wasn't easy for Brian Taylor to do what he did.

As a matter of fact, life itself is tough but it is rewarding—especially when you are tough on yourself. Take a page from Brian Taylor's book, keep on pumpin', and I'll certainly see you at the top!

Action Steps

1. Today I will be tougher on myself, because I know that if I keep on keeping on I can win!
2. Today I will_____

_____

Courage is resistance to fear, mastery of fear—not absence of fear.

113

. . . and Obstacles

Geri Jewell is a twenty-four-year-old girl with a severe case of cerebral palsy, and yet she is one of the hottest new stars in Hollywood. How did it happen?

Geri has a lot of courage. When she was a little girl she had a dream: she saw herself in a long, beautiful gown, walking straight, without cerebral palsy. Geri has persistently held to her dream, and she has worked very hard to make that dream come true. Somewhere along the way she decided to become a comedienne.

She had many obvious obstacles to overcome. At first it was almost impossible to get anyone to take her seriously as a performer, but she persisted and pursued her dream. She began performing at The Comedy Store in Los Angeles for free. It wasn't easy that first night, but Geri was able to use her handicap to her advantage. She quickly got the audience on her side and made them feel comfortable with her marvelous sense of humor. She was a hit and was invited back the next week.

Geri has now been on many television shows and is able to select parts that she wants. Like most people who make it in their chosen professions, Geri made it because she saw herself in her mind's eye doing exactly what she wanted to do. Her mind painted the picture and she put in the necessary work to complete that picture.

Action Steps

1. Today I will use my obstacles as stepping stones instead of stumbling blocks.
2. Today I will_____

_____

Never tell a young person that something cannot be done. God may have been waiting for centuries for somebody ignorant enough of the impossible to do that very thing.

Dr. J. A. Holmes

. . . and Miracles

She was told at eleven years of age that she'd never walk again. At twenty-two she walked the boardwalk as Miss America, 1980.

Cheryl Prewitt of Mississippi, Miss America in 1980, was in an automobile accident at age eleven. Her left leg was crushed and had to be patched with one hundred stitches. Doctors told her she would never walk again. While the damaged leg did eventually heal, it was significantly shorter than her healthy right leg.

However, at a revival meeting several years later, she saw her shortened left leg "grow two inches instantaneously!" She says she walked by a "miracle of God," but an equal miracle was and is her beautiful attitude.

Cheryl could have sat down and quit—many people would have. The obvious question is to ask where she got that marvelous direction and that beautiful attitude? Interestingly enough, a single incident before the accident had a direct impact on what she has been able to do with her life. At age five, in the little family-owned country store, the milkman one day looked at her and told her she was going to be Miss America. Cheryl believed him. From a single, powerful, positive thought, a positive attitude developed, and Miss America 1980 was born.

Words are the most powerful forces in the world. Positive words of love, hope, and encouragement can lift a person to new heights. Negative words of frustration, hatred, vulgarity, and despair can tear or bring a person down. So watch your language, folks.

Action Steps

1. Today I will speak only kind and positive words to _____ _____ and _____ .
2. Today I will_____
_____

She was not pretty, but she might have been handsome if somebody had kept telling her that she was pretty.

J. B. Priestley

. . . and Tough Jobs

*H*e took what no one else wanted and became the best. As a baseball player, he was the best at his position; a leader on the field and a powerful clutch-hitter who also hit for average. Unfortunately, a tragic accident shortened his career and left him partially paralyzed, in a wheelchair for the rest of his life. In his brief span on the diamond, however, he achieved enough success to be voted into the Baseball Hall of Fame. Of course, I'm talking about Roy Campanella, the great catcher for the old Brooklyn Dodgers.

The question is, why did Roy Campanella become a catcher in the first place? It is a difficult, injury-prone position. The answer is simple and intriguing: when Campanella was trying out for his high school team, his coach began separating players by position. Roy noticed that no one was standing in the catching area. It was immediately obvious to Roy that anybody who really wanted to play would have a pretty good shot at it in that position.

Since he really wanted to play baseball, Roy Campanella decided to be a catcher. He worked hard, and became the best player on the team, and got his future in baseball under way. What about his teammates, the guys who shunned the catcher's job for the more glamorous positions? I never heard of them, did you?

Roy Campanella took an unglamorous job and did it extremely well. If you will take the tough jobs—those things that others don't want to do—and will do them well, success will be yours.

Action Steps

1. Today I will take all tasks in stride and do them conscientiously.
2. Today I will _____

Keep your face to the sun and the shadows will fall behind.

. . . and Talent

*P*eter Strudwick's magnificent book, *Come Run with Me,* is about running—but far more importantly, it is about life. Since 1969, when Peter started jogging seriously, he has logged nearly twenty thousand miles of running in marathons and in training. Three times he participated in the Pike's Peak Marathon. He is currently training for a marathon over the summit of Africa's Kilimanjaro.

His story is one of the most incredible stories in the history of sports. The thing that makes the story so remarkable is the fact that Peter Strudwick was born with legs that end in stumps just past the ankles; a left hand that has only a thumb and one finger; and a right arm that stops at the wrist.

Peter Strudwick, called "Pete" by his friends, has accomplished feats of physical skill and endurance that absolutely confound logic. His story is an inspiration to all who read it. Surely we must feel that if Pete can do what he has done with what he has, each one of us can do *more* with what we have. Thanks, Pete, for being an inspiration to us.

Action Steps

1. Today I will reflect on the courage of Peter Strudwick and remember to count my blessings.
2. Today I will_____

_____

A great deal of talent is lost to the world for want of a little courage. Every day sends to their graves obscure men whom timidity prevented from making a first effort.

Sydney Smith

... and One Person

*C*an one student in a large high school really change anything?

Laurie Cox of Coronado High School in Scottsdale, Arizona, felt very strongly that the students should salute the flag and say the pledge of allegiance. She felt that if students saluted the flag on a daily basis they would be willing to defend the flag if the occasion arose.

Her principal and her teacher were not exactly overwhelmed with the idea. Her boyfriend was appalled, but Laurie had made up her mind. It took a lot of work, but she managed to get over three thousand signatures on a petition. Today in Coronado High School the students salute the flag and say the pledge of allegiance.

Laurie started the ball rolling, but three thousand other students showed that they *wanted* to demonstrate their patriotism and their love of country. They needed a leader, someone who would make a commitment and step forward.

The next time you have a tendency to get a little down on yourself, our country, or young people, give yourself a lift—think about Laurie Cox and those three thousand students in Scottsdale, Arizona.

Action Steps

1. Today I will remember that I can be a leader who encourages others to take the first step in a positive direction.
2. Today I will _____

By nothing do men show their character more than by the things they laugh at.
Johann Wolfgang von Goethe

118

. . . and Misfortune

*A*n operation took Darlene Loucks *off* her feet and put her *on* her feet. Here's the story.

Darlene Loucks of Los Angeles finished school only to the eighth grade and was married at age fifteen. The mother of eight children, she was working as a waitress when surgery took her off her feet. It was physically impossible for her to spend long hours in any job that required lots of standing, so she had to find some other source of income. Her education and business experience were limited, but like most of us, Darlene Loucks knew she had some skills which could be marketed with a little imagination. She put that imagination to work, hauled out her old sewing machine, and got busy.

Darlene approached a dress manufacturer and sold him on the idea that she could create beautiful samples for display in his showrooms. Not only did that manufacturer buy the idea, the response was so tremendous that a number of other manufacturers asked her to do the same thing for them.

Today Darlene Loucks has twenty-seven people working for her, her business is growing, and she's back on her feet—financially, that is. Her story is a beautiful example of free enterprise at its best in America. It should give you the feeling that if Darlene Loucks can do that much with her problems, you can do more with your opportunities.

Action Steps

1. Today I will spend some time "off my feet" and "on my knees," being thankful for my problems.
2. Today I will_____

_____

Let him not imagine who aims at greatness that all is lost by a single adverse case of fortune.

Archbishop Venn

. . . and Character

*C*haracter, according to Cavett Robert, is the ability to carry out a good resolution long after the emotion of the moment has passed. Character is a critically important quality in a world conditioned to believe that if something doesn't look good, smell good, taste good, and qualify as fun, you shouldn't be involved.

In this book I use a lot of descriptive adjectives such as *rewarding, fun,* and *exciting,* but not once will you ever hear me say that success is easy. In order to get all the rewards life offers, there are many occasions when you have to hang in there and tough it out.

Winston Churchill eloquently expressed this concept in his inspiring "Battle of Britain" radio broadcast. This speech literally picked up his nation by its bootstraps, and it saved both Britain and the free world in the process. He told them it would take blood, toil, tears and sweat to win. He didn't promise them the battle would be easy, but he did promise them victory.

I promise you the same thing. If you have the character to hang in there when it's tough, you will develop or acquire every other characteristic necessary to win in the game of life.

Action Steps

1. Today I will hang in there and tough out those difficult situations which arise.
2. Today I will_____

_____

Character is the ability to carry out a good resolution long after the emotion of the moment has passed.

Cavett Robert

. . . and Disease

*T*his might strike you as being unusual, but polio, pneumonia, and twelve hours daily in an iron lung can equal outstanding success. Richard Chavez is a thirty-six-year-old teacher and spokesman for the Disadvantaged People of America. A Mexican-American from Los Angeles, he was stricken with polio and pneumonia at age five.

Since then, however, he has built one of the most innovative training schools in America for the handicapped and disadvantaged. Besides his own personal handicaps, Chavez has also overcome economic adversity, a language barrier, and nearly ten years of employment rejections and put-downs.

His institute, which he founded in 1973, has trained more than six thousand underprivileged high school dropouts, workmen's compensation clients, former law offenders, mental health patients, former drug addicts, and alcoholics. More than eighty-eight percent of his students, feeling good about themselves and their capabilities, leave Chavez to go into permanent, unsubsidized employment. That is fantastic!

Our hats are off to Richard Chavez. Surely if he, with all his adversities, can move his personal mountains and make a success of his life, all of us can overcome the little molehills that stand in our pathways to accomplishment.

Action Steps

1. Today I will recognize my mountains as none other than molehills, and will take action to reduce them even further.
2. Today I will_____

_____

If you brood over your troubles, you will have a perfect hatch.

. . . Against All Odds

*T*he young teenager was distraught. The doctor had rendered the verdict: you can't play football, baseball, or any of the regular athletic events that teenagers generally participate in. Every day, though, the young boy rode past a golf course. He started to think that *maybe* he could do that, but the doctor was adamant. "You don't understand. You can't play golf on crutches!"

The youngster persisted, and he started going to the golf course. He would ride a cart, hobble over to the spot where his ball was, lay the crutches down, and then hit the ball. Day after day he did this, until he began to notice that his legs were getting stronger.

Eventually the persistent golfer abandoned the cart and threw away the crutches. In 1978, as a result of the years of patient, constant, optimistic effort, Andy North won the United States Open Golf Tournament. The person who had been told he could never participate in sports won not because of his great natural athletic ability, but because of his patient, persistent effort and a firm conviction that if he kept at it he was going to win. Andy North is a winner, and with the same commitment, *you* can be a winner!

Action Steps

1. Today I will remember that if Andy North, although crippled by a bone disease, can accomplish his goals, then I can accomplish mine too.
2. Today I will_____

Keep your fears for yourself, but share your courage with others.
                                                    Robert Louis Stevenson

. . . and Skill

You've heard it said a thousand times that anything worth doing is worth doing well. But Steve Brown, from Atlanta, Georgia, says, "Anything worth doing is worth doing poorly." He elaborates by explaining that if something is worth doing, you've got to understand that it's going to take time and effort to do it well. In the initial stages we simply might not be very good at it. However, even though we might at first do it poorly, if we study new methods, procedures, and techniques for doing the work better, and then make the extra effort to hone our skills, we will get better and better until eventually we will be doing the project very well.

Let me say it again. Anything worth doing is worth doing poorly. Start from where you are with what you have and give it your best shot. Even though it might not be the shot of an expert, if you hang in there and hone your skills with lots of hard work and practice, you will eventually be good and maybe even will be an expert!

Action Steps

1. Today I will remember that anything worth doing is worth doing poorly until I learn to do it well.
2. Today I will_____

_____

By the mile it's a trial; by the yard it's hard; but by the inch it's a cinch!

. . . and the Field Goal Kicker

S teve Little was a fierce competitor on the football field, and now he's fighting a battle of a different kind. Steve tied the NCAA field goal record at the University of Arkansas and was drafted number one by the St. Louis Cardinals football team in 1978. He was under great pressure from the very beginning, and even though he had some great moments (a fifty-two yard field goal against the Dallas Cowboys was one) he struggled and finally lost his job to another kicker.

Only eight hours after he was cut from the team, Steve was in an automobile accident that paralyzed him from the neck down. Now he is fighting a far more serious battle than his football days. Is he bitter? Absolutely not! Steve is proving to be a winner through his great attitude. He believes that he will make the best of this situation, and that through his handling of this challenge he will inspire other people to handle the tragedies of their lives.

Steve Little is still battling. He knows he might never walk again, but his courage, attitude, and desire to help others make him a real winner. There are some events in life that we cannot change, but we do have a say in determining our response to those events!

Action Steps

1. Today I will courageously face my battles with Steve Little as my inspiration.
2. Today I will_____

_____

The right attitude and one arm will beat the wrong attitude and two arms every time.

David Schwartz

. . . and Age

*I*f you had been a baseball fan in the 1930s, you might have seen Hub Kittle pitch in the minor leagues. There is also a possibility that your grandson could have seen him pitch in the 1980s. That's right, Hub Kittle is the only man alive to have pitched in professional baseball games across six decades.

Kittle began his career way back in 1936 with the Chicago Cubs. He pitched in the minor leagues during the thirties and forties, but he finally decided that he had had enough during the fifties. His love for baseball kept him in the game, though; he became one of the finest pitching coaches in professional baseball.

In 1969, while coaching for the Savannah, Georgia, team, a shortage of pitchers forced him into a game. And in 1973, while serving as pitching coach for the Houston Astros, Manager Leo Durocher called upon Kittle to protect a one-run lead in an exhibition game against the Detroit Tigers. Hub pitched a scoreless inning and got the save.

His chance to take the mound came again in the 1980s. At the young age of sixty-three, while serving as pitching coach for the Springfield Redbirds, Hub Kittle pitched one inning. At that point he became the only player in the history of the American pastime to play in baseball games that spanned over six decades. Hub Kittle has definitely proven the old saying, "You are as old as you think you are."

Action Steps

1. Today I will use my age as an asset rather than an excuse.
2. Today I will_____

It is not by the gray of the hair that one knows the age of the heart.
                                                          Edward Bulwer-Lytton

---

Goals . . .

Success consists of a series of little daily victories.

. . . and Effort

*W*hen football player Aubrey Shultz walked into head coach Grant Teaff's office at Baylor University, he discussed three goals:

Number one: he wanted to be an All-Southwest Conference center.
Number two: he wanted to be an All-American.
Number three: he wanted Baylor to win the Southwest Conference Football Championship.

However, each of his three goals had a parallel difficulty:

Number one: he was a guard—not a center.
Number two: he was at second string hardly an All-American prospect.
Number three: Baylor hadn't won the Southwest Conference in *fifty years.*

But Aubrey worked hard. He lifted weights, ate the right food, and gained the thirty-five pounds the coach told him he needed to gain. By spring training he moved to center; by the first of the season he was a starter. By the end of the season, Aubrey Shultz was named All-Southwest Conference and All-American, and led Baylor to its first Southwest Conference Championship in half a century. Coach Teaff says, "Aubrey is a winner. Not for his titles, but because he thought the impossible was possible and wasn't afraid to set high goals."

Action Steps

1. Today I will seek the counsel of the wise who can help me reach my goals.
2. Today I will_____

_____

The difference between great and good is a little extra effort.
Clarence "Biggie" Munn

. . . and Wishes

*H*ow can you get what you really want in life? I believe you start by determining what you *really* want and then establishing a plan to achieve it.

Barbara Sher wrote a book entitled, *Wishcraft: How to Get What You Really Want.* That's right, *wish*craft is what she stresses as the key to obtaining wants. She suggests that you need pencil, paper, and a problem. The next step is to complete the sentence, "I can't reach my goal because . . ." For example, you might say that you can't reach your goal because you don't have the credentials, money, or experience.

Barbara Sher says that once you've determined what keeps you from reaching your goal, you answer one of two questions about that barrier to success. 1. How can I reach my goal *without* . . . ? 2. How can I *get* . . . ? I have a great story about how this method works.

Jean Nidetch wasn't a doctor or nutritionist, she was just a lady who wanted to be thin. She successfully lost the weight that she wanted to lose, so she set a goal to help others lose weight. Her obstacle was that she was not a recognized authority in the field of weight control. Jean decided to design a package that conveyed to others that she knew what they were going through, that she understood, because she was just like them, only thinner. She turned her goal into a multi-million dollar business— Weight Watchers—despite the obstacles she faced. Jean Nidetch reached her goal because she had a plan and followed a procedure. Decide what you want, develop a plan to reach your goal, follow through, and the odds are great that you too will succeed.

Action Steps

1. Today I will determine what I really want—just for today—and will develop a plan for achievement.
2. Today I will _____

The best preparation for tomorrow is to do today's work superbly well.
William Osler

. . . and Time

*T*he millionaire and the pauper are alike in at least one respect—each one is given 1,440 minutes of time every day. Yet most people constantly complain that they don't have enough time.

Proper time management is a must for every successful person. Time is our most important commodity. When those moments and hours slip away they do not return; they are gone forever. The question is how do you effectively use your time?

You start to answer the question of time management with the realization that there *aren't* sixty minutes in every hour. As a practical matter, there are only as many minutes in the hour as you *use*.

How many hours are you wasting? If you really want to know you will take a serious inventory. Use a calendar or appointment book and mark it off in eight-hour slots. Now mark off the hours into sixty-minute segments. As you go through each day this week, keep track of where your time is going by writing down what you do during those sixty-minute time frames. Do it for one week. Then go back and check your book. You'll be surprised when you realize that hours and hours of time are wasted on nonessential items due to procrastination and poor organization.

After you've thought about your use of time allotted to you, try the time inventory again. This time plan your week more carefully. Fill those time slots with correspondence, phone calls, or follow-ups. Always have a folder of things to do at a moment's notice.

Remember that time really is the only thing you have to sell to yourself or anyone else. The better use you make of your time, the higher the price you will be paid for it.

Action Steps

1. Today I will begin a one-week inventory of how I am "spending" my time.
2. Today I will_____

_____

> *Americans have more time-saving devices and less time than any other group of people in the world.*
>
> Duncan Caldwell

. . . and Planning

*E*verybody wants to be a success, but most folk don't know what to do or where to start. One prerequisite for success is establishing a goal. A second essential for winning in life is developing a plan to reach your goal. These essentials apply regardless of whether your interests and goals are in education, medicine, politics, athletics—or whatever.

A famous actor decided to make a midlife career change. His goal was to enter politics. He carefully charted a plan that began with involvement in local and then in state politics. That man, whose plan also included the highest possible office in America, is Ronald Reagan.

A small boy who wore glasses decided that he wanted to be a great professional golf player. He played in high school, college, and is now one of the all-time money winners on the PGA tour. His name is Tom Kite.

Goals are not reached by merely thinking about them. There must be a clear-cut plan of action. A part of successfully achieving your goal is not only working hard, but also working *accurately* toward your goal. People who reach great heights of success are those who carefully lay out a definite plan to do so. They not only set a goal, but also establish a course of action to reach that goal.

Action Steps

1. Today I will identify those goals worthy of my maximum efforts.
2. Today I will develop at least one detailed plan of action for one of my goals.
3. Today I will_____

_____

The poorest of all men is the one without a dream.

. . . and Adversity

*D*avid Welsh was determined to be a lawyer. The only problem was that he had dyslexia, a learning disability that causes letters to appear exactly the opposite of the way they should.

In elementary school, David's parents spent long hours reading his class assignments to him. He dictated his answers to them, and they typed them out. No doubt, many shook their heads at David's dream to become an attorney.

David entered Westminster College and taped his classes on a recorder rather than taking notes. He typed all of his examinations. David graduated from college. No doubt several shook their heads at his ambition to enter law school.

But David Welsh is a positive thinker. He entered the University of Tulsa Law School and recorded every lecture, listening to each again and again. He spent hours in the legal library reading his assignments, painstakingly working through them word by word. He dictated term papers and even dictated exam answers, all at his own expense.

Today, David Welsh is an attorney. Was it hard? Yes! Were there problems? Absolutely. Many told him he couldn't do it. But David's dream was to become an attorney, and he was willing to do what was necessary to make that dream come true.

I have a question: what's keeping you from your goals? On second thought, don't tell me about your obstacles, tell David Welsh—if you can catch him. At the moment he's pretty busy reaching for other goals. Look past the obstacles to your goal and you too can be an achiever!

Action Steps

1. Today I will concentrate on solutions, not problems.
2. Today I will_____

Character is not made in a crisis—it is only exhibited.

Robert Freeman

. . . and Opportunity

*A*n obstacle is simply an opportunity for growth and improvement. A few years ago Gary Goranson decided to trade in the family car for a newer model. It was in excellent condition except for one problem—the paint job. The car looked ten years older than it actually was. He couldn't get what he felt the car was worth because no one wanted a car that looked worn out.

Since Gary is not the type of person to give up easily, he began to look around at different methods for shining up the paint jobs on cars. Before long he discovered a method that provided remarkable results.

Gary bought an old machine originally used by the Canadian Air Force for cleaning aircraft. It rotated like the human hand, only much faster, at several hundred revolutions per minute. With this machine he was not only able to put a fantastic new shine on his car, he was soon doing the same for friends. Seeing the obvious possibilities, Gary Goranson bought several of the machines and founded Tidy Car, a business specializing in car appearance. He now has hundreds of franchises.

This is one example of how a small obstacle turned into the business opportunity of a lifetime. It is also an excellent example of understanding the business relation between your problems and the problems of other people. When you solve a problem you have, your rewards will come in direct proportion to the number of other people who are helped by your solution.

Action Steps

1. Today I will look for ways to turn lemons into lemonade.
2. Today I will_____

The daily grind is what gives a man polish.

133

. . . and Fear

"*T*here is always fear. The trick is not to eliminate it but to overcome it," says Peter Vidmar, who grew up in Los Angeles loving sports, but very frustrated because of his size. According to Peter, "It was hard for me to be an asset to a team. I was more like a liability."

When he was eleven years old, Peter decided to try gymnastics. Inspired by Olga Korbut and Nadia Comaneci, he continued gymnastics through high school and into college at UCLA, where he received a scholarship. Peter Vidmar is currently the top-ranking American in world-class gymnastic competition. He recently captured the prestigious America Cup, with an amazing fifty-nine points out of a possible sixty points in six events—the highest American score ever. Yet Peter Vidmar is only twenty-one years old and five feet, five inches tall.

Peter's coach recently made this surprising statement to *People* magazine. "Peter is not particularly talented. I've had boys who were more gifted physically, with more kinetic awareness, strength, and flexibility. But Peter could surpass them all because of his *singular determination.*" Peter was so determined, his coach recalls, that he practiced on a stunt for *four years* before he could successfully perform it. I'm convinced that if you will go after your goals with the determination of Peter Vidmar, I *will* see you at the top!

Action Steps

1. Today I will focus my energies on the number-one activity that will help me to succeed. This activity is _____

    _____.

2. Today I will_____

    _____

Concentrate all your thoughts upon the work in hand. The sun's rays do not burn until brought to a focus.

Alexander Graham Bell

134

. . . Overcoming Obstacles

*C*arol Farmer found out after only two semesters of teaching that education wasn't for her. But what else could she do?

She wanted to be a designer, so she set a goal to make more money her first year as a freelance designer than she had made teaching. Carol Farmer had made $5,000 teaching; she made $5,012 her first year as a designer.

Her freelance business grew into an ad agency. She was soon offered a salary increase to thirty-five thousand dollars, but she turned it down to form her own company. The former teacher made over one hundred thousand dollars in her first year, twenty times more than she had made less than ten years previously and five times more than she had made the year before.

In 1976, Carol Farmer formed the Doody Company, which billed over $15 million in its first three years. Her staff increased from six to two hundred. Carol Farmer continues to diversify. She recently accepted an invitation to share her business success with scholars at Harvard University.

Too often people see obstacles as roadblocks instead of opportunities. Carol Farmer turned disappointment and unhappiness in one career into happiness, creativity, and profit in another career. Join Carol Farmer in approaching obstacles creatively, and I'll see you at the top!

Action Steps

1. Today I will spell "obstacle" as "opportunity," and I will look for answers instead of more obstacles.
2. Today I will_____

_____

Small opportunities are often the beginning of great enterprises.

Demosthenes

135

. . . and Challenges

*L*ife is truly what you make it. On June 4, 1983, UPI and AP each carried a heartwarming story about graduation. Both accounts reaffirm the principle that life is truly what you make it.

Associated Press told the story of Dung Nguyen. When she arrived in the United States from Vietnam in 1975, she could only speak *one* word of English. In June of 1983, Dung Nguyen graduated as valedictorian of her high school class in Pensacola, Florida. President Reagan phoned to congratulate her for her academic accomplishments.

United Press International told the story of Geraldine Lawhorn. Geraldine Lawhorn is one of the older graduates of the class of '83 from Northeastern Illinois University. Geraldine is blind and deaf—in fact, she became only the sixth deaf and blind person to graduate from college. When Geraldine was asked about her remarkable achievement, she replied, "We all have the same goals, but we have to go on different roads."

Dung Nguyen and Geraldine Lawhorn didn't give up. They excelled in spite of the obstacles. The exciting thing about their stories is that if Dung Nguyen and Geraldine Lawhorn can reach their goals despite the challenges, *you* can reach your goals too!

Action Steps

1. Today I will remember that my obstacles cannot keep me from my goal—only I can do that!
2. Today I will_____

God gives every bird its food, but He does not throw it into the nest.

J. G. Holland

. . . and Saying "No"

*D*oes the word *no* sound like a negative word to you? Of course it does. But there are times when "no" actually means "yes" to success.

Fourteen-year-old Sandra played a magnificent melody on the piano as the crowd sat quietly and admired her talent. As she finished the song she received rousing applause. Sandra had received her reward; not only did she feel the inner satisfaction of knowing that she had played well, she was offered the appreciation of the audience as well.

Sandra's skill did not come easy. She has worked more than four hours each day for nine long years in order to play the piano the way she now plays. During those years she said "no" to many parties, social activities, silly television shows, pointless movies, and hundreds of other time-consuming activities in order to sit home alone and practice.

When Sandra says "no" to those time-wasting activities, she is saying "yes" to a much more important goal in her life. There you have it: sometimes "no" actually means "yes" to success.

Action Steps

1. Today I will say "no" to failure and "yes" to success.
2. Today I will_____

_____

> *Those who make the worst use of their time are the first to complain of its shortness.*
>
> Jean de La Bruyère

137

. . . and Work

*W*omen might have to work harder to get to the top, but Roxanne Mankin says it's worth it. Roxanne is president of her own company and makes four hundred thousand dollars a year. She is a most attractive woman, and she is a lady with a mind and a will. Her life is consumed by ferocious self-discipline, isolation, and work. She has advanced in position from secretary to executive in less than ten years. She neither smokes nor drinks; she works fifteen hours a day, spends hours on airplanes, is working on an M.B.A., and loves real estate.

Why does she push so hard? She says it's not for the money anymore, but for the love of the field of real estate, the intricacies in financing, and the social dimensions involved. There are many factors involved in a success story such as that of Roxanne Mankin but there are two matters that explain much of her success. She loves to help the elderly, and she feels a responsibility to other women.

Roxanne set her goals, worked with intense desire, and now she has made it. Has it been worth the hardships and the discipline? Roxanne Mankin, like most successful people, emphatically says "*yes.*" She clearly appreciates the fact that you don't "pay the price" to succeed, you enjoy the price of success.

Action Steps

1. Today I will remind myself that anything worth having is worth working for—and then I will go to *work!*
2. Today I will_____

_____

Some people think they are overworked because it takes them all day to do a three-hour job.

138

. . . and Priorities

Setting priorities is fairly easy, but it does require thought and planning. We shouldn't have any trouble setting priorities. All we have to do is list the things we need to do and rank them in the order of their importance. Simple? Yes. Easy? Maybe.

Let's suppose you have three activities that need to have priorities set. Suppose you need to buy a flea collar for the dog, to shop for a new car, and to take the baby to the doctor. Prioritize these from one to three, and the priorities seem clear. But what if you're just taking the baby to the doctor for a checkup, and the car is fine (you just want a new one)? Those fleas on your dog, having a picnic at your expense and possibly even munching on *you,* assume a new importance. Priority number one becomes getting that flea collar.

It's good to make long-range plans, but as a practical matter it's also *necessary* to think about matters that demand attention now. Careful planning allows you to have time for both.

In your planning for tomorrow, don't neglect today. It's too valuable, and there are exactly the same number of hours in the day today as there will be tomorrow. Sometimes the discipline of dealing successfully with short term crises today will prepare you to reach those long range goals tomorrow.

Action Steps

1. Today I will give consideration to my priorities—both short-term and long-range. My top three short-range priorities are:
   1. _____ 2. _____
   _____ 3. _____
   My top three long-range priorities are: 1. _____
   2. _____ 3. _____
2. Today I will_____
   _____

It takes as much energy to wish as it does to plan.

. . . and Simplicity

*T*oshihiko Seko has a simple training program. It's so simple, he tells it in only twelve words. And yet with this plan, Toshihiko won the 1981 Boston Marathon and the 1983 Tokyo Marathon. This plan enabled him to outrun the world's greatest, fastest, and most gifted runners. What is his plan? Seko says, "I run ten kilometers in the morning and twenty in the evening." When Seko was told that his plan seemed too simple when compared to that of other marathoners, he replied, "The plan *is* simple. But I do it *every single day,* 365 days a year."

I believe people fail to reach their goals not because their plans are too simple, but because they aren't willing to follow their plans! Many goals do not require detailed plans. But they do require *following* the plan.

Making an A requires time spent in study instead of watching the soaps, comedies, detective shows, ten o'clock news, and late-night reruns on the night before the test. Playing the piano involves daily practice. Losing weight requires a daily program of exercise and sensible eating.

Seko's plan was effective because he followed it every day. Plans don't have to be complicated but they *do* have to be followed.

Action Steps

1. Today I will plan my work *and* work my plan!
2. Today I will_____

There is no pleasure in having nothing to do; the fun is in having lots to do and doing it.

. . . and Ingredients

*I*f you were looking for an improbable success story you would probably choose this one.

He was sixty-five years old and broke. He owned a house and a beat-up car, and received a Social Security check of $105. But he also had a dream and a secret method of preparing fried chicken. After spending a lifetime in the restaurant business, his dream was to franchise his recipe.

He left his home in Kentucky and started traveling in other states to sell his idea. No one was interested in Missouri, Indiana, Illinois, Kansas; he traveled all the way to Salt Lake City, Utah, before he made his first sale. But his special formula soon became a hit. Within a short time, hundreds of restaurants all over the country were selling chicken that was "finger-lickin' good." The man was Colonel Harlan Sanders.

A dream, a plan, and hard work were the ingredients the Colonel used to turn his dream into reality. But this is no secret formula! These same ingredients are available to you: a dream, a plan, and hard work. With this recipe, you can turn your dream into a reality. It probably won't be easy, but my observation is that it is more fun to succeed than it is to fail.

Action Steps

1. Today I will list the six most important Action Steps to take tomorrow.
2. Today I will_____

_____

Don't discourage the other man's plans unless you have better ones to offer.

. . . and Hope

*J*une Dutton penned, "Hope is a handful of dreams. Hope is a patient heart. Hope is a cure for sadness . . . a mender of broken hearts. Hope is the strength to persevere." I would like to add that hope is Dennis Walters.

Dennis Walters was one of the most promising young golfers in the country until disaster struck. In 1974 he was involved in a freak golf cart accident that paralyzed both his legs.

But Dennis was not content to *watch* golf; his goal was to be a golf instructor! Now that's quite a goal for a person with paralyzed legs. Dennis learned how to hit golf balls from a sitting position. He designed a swivel seat for his golf cart. He learned how to leave the golf cart by walking with crutches and then to putt with one hand.

Today thirty-year-old Dennis Walters plays eighteen holes in the low seventies. He drives 250 yards from a sitting position. He's not only a golf instructor in Florida, but he is also one of only four players in the United States who can make a living from golf exhibitions.

Dennis Walters is a man with hope. What he has done gives all of us hope!

Action Steps

1. Today I will remember that as long as I have hope, all is *not* lost!
2. Today I will_____

Hope is the strength to persevere.

June Dutton

142

. . . and Work

*O*ften the difference between success and failure is simply desire. The halfback with the football, the salesman with his product, the mother with her children, or the student with his lessons—all must have a deep desire to excel.

Of all the factors that help lead to success (and there are many!) perhaps nothing is more important than simple raw desire and determination to succeed. The football player running with the football must have a one-track determination to get to the goal line. The marathon runner who runs for more than two hours has a lot of time to think while running, and he or she must have tremendous single-minded desire. The mother who spends twenty-four hours each day with her little ones must have lots of love and a tremendous desire to give her children the best possible preparation for life.

The salesman who goes out each day to sell his product is also one who must have desire. He must know the right sales techniques, know his product and believe in it, have some knowledge of his prospective customer, and know how to give his sales presentation. But unless the salesman truly has the desire to sell, he will not be successful.

The salesman can know all the techniques involved, the halfback can be a fast runner, the mother can have all the answers, the marathoner can be in great shape, but without an overwhelming desire to succeed each one will not climb as high as his or her ability actually allows. What about you? Are you pursuing that deep-down desire of your life? Are you striving toward the goal of your choice? If you will, then I truly will see you at the top!

Action Steps

1. Today I will eliminate distractions and place my tasks in order of importance or priority, and I will work, work, *work!*
2. Today I will_____

_____

> *I want to be thoroughly used up when I die, for the harder I work, the more I live.*
>
> George Bernard Shaw

. . . and the Formula

I have a very important question! Do you have a wish-book in your life?

As a child in Depression-crippled America, I often took the Sears, Roebuck catalog, flipped the pages, and wished I had this toy, this bicycle, this particular garment, this rifle, and so on for thousands of other things. I dreamed that someday I would be able to own all of them.

I'm personally convinced that every one of us, regardless of age, needs his or her own wish-book. However, in order for those wishes to become reality, a person must make plans and take specific action. Here are seven steps you need to take in order to get your wishes or reach your goals.

First, identify what you want. Second, clearly spell out why you want to reach that particular goal. Third, list the obstacles that stand between you and your goal. Fourth, identify the growth process—the things you need to know—in order to get to your goal. Fifth, identify the people you need to work with to reach your goal. Sixth, develop a detailed plan of action to reach success. Seventh, set a date on when you expect to reach that goal. These seven specific steps will move you from the "wish-book" stage to the "accomplishing" stage of your path to success.

Action Steps

1. Today I will take one of my dreams from my own "wish book," apply the seven-step formula to that dream, and turn it into reality.
2. Today I will_____

_____

You must have long-range goals to keep you from being frustrated by short-range failure.

Charles C. Noble

. . . and Concentration

*T*he present day is important to you for this reason: you can waste it or use it, but no matter how you spend it, you've traded a day of *your* life for it! I have three suggestions for using your time more efficiently.

The first is to devote time to your goals. Bob Richards, a former Olympic pole vault champion, said that he spent over ten thousand hours practicing the pole vault. After the Olympics, Bob accurately observed that a person can be good at anything he puts ten thousand hours into. *You* can be good at anything *you* put ten thousand hours into.

Second, take advantage of the time you have. Herbert Hoover wrote a book during the time he spent waiting in railroad stations. Noel Coward wrote his popular song, "I'll See You Again," while caught in a traffic jam.

Finally, don't waste your time. A popular magazine recently conducted a time study of eighteen executives in fourteen companies. They found that these executives spent an average of five and one-half hours a day in conversation. The conclusion was that executives have enough time to accomplish their goals, they just don't use it.

Each of us has just as much time available as Tolstoy did when he wrote *War and Peace.* Each of us has just as much time as Edison had when he invented the light bulb. This *is* an important day! No matter how you spend it, you've traded a day of your life for it.

Action Steps

1. Today I will realize that I am trading a day of my life for the time that I am spending. I will spend my time wisely and take advantage of the time that I have by devoting it toward achieving my goals.
2. Today I will_____

_____

We cannot pause, or hesitate, or kill time—as if you could kill time without injuring eternity.

Joseph C. Grew

. . . and Women

*W*ith more and more women entering the job market today, the question we have to ask is: "Are problems in business any different for women than for men?"

Yes indeed, women are different! And for that we men will always be grateful. However, there are many areas in which both men and women should have the same attitudes. Success principles are the same for women as they are for men, but none of these principles work unless those that use them know exactly where they are going.

This means that a person shouldn't launch into a new career unless he—or she!—has a clear-cut plan of the goals that are to be accomplished. According to Helen McLane, vice president of an executive search firm, women are less likely to have career plans. It is very important for any person on the way to the top—male or female—to set priorities, establish a time frame, and have a clear definition of what is to be accomplished.

All of us must have a definite plan of action, but this is especially true of women who are entering the career marketplace for the first time. Think out your plan and define your goal.

Action Steps

1. Today I will spend _____ minutes or _____ hours in planning.
2. Today I will_____

_____

Shallow men [and women] believe in luck; wise and strong men [and women] believe in cause and effect.

Ralph Waldo Emerson

. . . and Fatigue

On July 4, 1952, Florence Chadwick stepped into the water off Catalina Island and headed for the California coast twenty-one miles away. Fatigue set in as the hours ticked off, but her big problem was the bone-chilling cold of the water. Fifteen hours later, numb with cold, she asked to be taken out of the water. A short time later she learned that she'd been pulled out only a half-mile from the coast. She reflected that she could have whipped the cold and the fatigue if she just could have seen the land, if only the fog had not obscured her goal. It blinded her reasoning, her eyes, and her heart. This was the only time Florence Chadwick ever quit.

Two months later she swam that same channel. Again fog obscured her view, but this time she swam with her faith intact. Somewhere behind that fog was land. Not only was Florence Chadwick the first woman to swim the Catalina Channel; she beat the men's record by two hours.

The message is clear: you might not be able to see the end of the tunnel, but it *is* there! So decide that the goal you seek is there—even if you can't see it. If you will commit yourself to your goal in spite of your fatigue, your chances of reaching your goal will be dramatically increased!

Action Steps

1. Today I will remember that the end of the tunnel—my goal—is within reach, even if I can't see it. I will therefore refuse to give up!
2. Today I will_____

_____

Go as far as you can see, and when you get there you will always be able to see farther.

. . . and Action

*B*enjamin Disraeli, the famous prime minister of England of another era, pointed out that while action might not always bring happiness, there is no happiness without action. Aruskind said the same truth another way. "Doing is the great thing, for if people do what is right, in time they come to like doing it." Dale Carnegie emphatically stated, "If you want to be enthusiastic, you've got to *act* enthusiastic." For William James, attitude is caused by action: "We do not sing because we are happy; we are happy because we sing."

All of these men are saying the same thing. Activity, action, or doing something will bring not only rewards and recognition, but will bring happiness as well. When we are busy doing things, we occupy our minds in constructive ways. Deep down the knowledge that we are accomplishing tasks brings a sense of self-satisfaction and happiness that can be found in no other manner. So the rule appears to be a simple one: If happiness is what you seek, you've got to work for it—actively!

Action Steps

1. Today I will remember that *action* is my key to accomplishment.
2. Today I will_____

_____

Logic will not change an emotion, but action will!

. . . and Breaks

*T*here are many who go sailing through the game of life with the mistaken notion that, unless you get good breaks, you will not be successful. My own observation, however, has been that ninety-nine percent of the people who get breaks *make* those breaks.

Years ago Gibbon noted, "The winds and waves are always on the side of the ablest navigators." Later, someone else rephrased that in a more modern—and perhaps a little more cynical—fashion: "The race does not always go to the strong and to the swift, but that is the way to bet." You might explain this talk about good breaks by saying that the best way to win the race is to prepare to win the race. The best way to get to the top is to get to the bottom of things with conscientious preparation and effort.

"There is no such thing as a favorable trade wind if you have no idea where you're going." The point that these thinkers are making is that you should decide what you want, work diligently to prepare to reach your objectives, and finally, expect to reach those objectives. Excellent advice from these men of the past!

Action Steps

1. Today I will *make* my breaks by preparing conscientiously, with sustained effort.
2. Today I will_____

> *You can do it gradually—day by day and play by play—if you* want *to do it, if you* will *to do it, if you* work *to do it over a sufficiently long period of time.*
> William E. Holl

. . . and Leadership

As a young salesman I had the advantage of having a dedicated man, who was much like an older brother, as my sales manager. His name was Bill Cranford, and he had the proverbial patience of Job with me—a struggling, inept young nonproducer.

When I finally learned to survive in the world of selling and started to move up in management, Bill taught me a very simple lesson in leadership. He took a piece of string and said, "Zig, this piece of string would be tough to push, but it's easy to pull. People are pretty much that way—easy to lead, but hard to push. As you move up into management, Zig, you'll discover that if you'll set the example and provide the leadership for your people, you won't have to do much pushing. They'll be delighted to follow the leader."

From my own personal experience over the years, I can tell you Bill was right. People *are* delighted to follow the leader. This is true whether we are talking about leadership in sales, family, business, church, or politics. Lead rather than push, and you—as well as those around you—will move toward accomplishing goals!

Action Steps

1. Today I will remember that I can accomplish much more by asking people to come with me than I can by pushing them out in front of me.
2. Today I will_____

_____

You can preach a better sermon with your life than with your lips.
Oliver Goldsmith

. . . and Three Important Qualities

I am a firm believer in goal-setting and in working hard long hours to reach goals. But there are times when goal-setting does not work. Goals are useless if they are unrealistic, immeasurable, or unchallenging. In order for goal-setting to be a successful part of your life or business, your objectives must have three qualities.

First, your goals must be realistic. It is an admirable attitude to set for yourself the goal of painting the counterpart to the Mona Lisa, but if you flunk Art 101, it is not a realistic goal.

Second, your goal must be measurable. For example, it would be difficult to set the goal that everyone in your business feel better in the office. A worthy ambition, yes; but as a goal it is useless because it is immeasurable.

Finally, your goal must be challenging. Not only must it be realistic, as we said, but it must also be a real challenge. Your goal must be out of reach but not out of sight. You need the energy that is generated by an exciting challenge, a mountain that is high enough so that the climbing will prove to be very, very rewarding!

Action Steps

1. Today I will make sure that my goals are realistic, measurable, and challenging!
2. Today I will_____

_____

Man's reach should exceed his grasp, or what is a heaven for?

151

. . . and Seeing the Reaching

I've been promoting the power of positive thinking for a long time. I have solid evidence that you will perform exactly as you program your mind to perform. You do this by mentally *seeing* the end result before you take the physical action. Jack Nicklaus *sees* the golf ball in the cup *before* he putts. Rafael Septien *sees* the ball sailing through the uprights *before* he kicks. Moses Malone *sees* the ball swishing through the net *before* he shoots.

Dr. Maxwell Maltz, in his excellent book *Psychocybernetics,* reports scientific research about the "mental training" that athletes often use. Tests have shown that basketball players who actually practiced free throws had only a slight edge over those who practiced primarily in the "mind's eye."

This process works for great athletes and it will work for you in your everyday behavior. You can code your mind to think like a winner, which is the first and most important step in becoming a winner. Practice positive thinking and positive projection, and the picture you paint in your mind will become a part of your performance!

Action Steps

1. Today I will *see* myself performing as a winner in all activities *before* I actually begin the activities.
2. Today I will_____

Man's mind—stretched by a new idea—never goes back to its original dimensions.

Oliver Wendell Holmes

How To . . .

The great aim of education is not knowledge but action.
Herbert Spencer

... Tolerate

I've spent a lot of time these past few years in airplanes, and I am always amazed at the capability of those mammoth machines to fly swiftly and safely through the air. Sometimes in rough weather you can see the wing tips flapping like those of an excited hawk.

On one such occasion a young fellow sitting next to me said excitedly, "Look, the wings are about to break off!" The flight attendant, who was standing nearby, calmly assured the man that the wings were made purposely to be flexible in rough weather. Engineers call that factor "tolerance." If the wings were made rigid they would not be able to withstand the pressures of quickly shifting air currents; in that case they certainly would snap like dry twigs in bad weather.

The ability to be flexible is very important to people as well. We must learn to adjust, to have tolerance in many ways.

Ask yourself these questions: "Do I have the ability to adjust? Do I have a healthy tolerance level? Am I flexible enough to bend so that I won't break?" Learn to roll with the storms of life and I'll see you at the top!

Action Steps

1. Today I will be flexible enough to bend, tolerant of others, and open to new ideas without compromising my basic beliefs.
2. Today I will_____

_____

Toleration is good for all, or it is good for none.

Edmund Burke

. . . Handle Opportunity

*I*t was Shakespeare who said, "We must take the current when it serves, or lose our venture." One dictionary definition talks about opportunity as a "fit" time. Opportunity is also defined as a chance for advancement or progress. Notice the word *chance* in that definition. Nothing in life includes an absolute guarantee, and opportunity is no exception. However, we often make our own breaks by seeing opportunities when others do not. How do we recognize opportunity? Here are a few tips that might help.

First, keep your eyes open for new ideas, new products, or new slants on old products. There is always another Hula-Hoop or another Frisbee idea just waiting to be discovered.

Second, don't leap before you take a good, long look. There is a proper balance between trying to cash in on new opportunity and being plain irrational about every new idea.

Third, don't overlook the opportunities right in your own company or office. For example, look around yourself—what is the biggest headache for your boss? Can you solve that problem? Commit your thoughts and ideas to writing in a clear and logical manner and present them to your boss.

Action Steps

1. Today I will be a "problem-solver" for those closest to me.
2. Today I will_____

_____

We must take the current when it serves, or lose our venture.

Shakespeare

156

. . . Accept

*C*hances are good that you have a friend or family member who has at least one mannerism that drives you up the wall. Perhaps you put up with it for a long time, until one day when you can't take it any more, and then you say everything you've been wanting to say in exactly the wrong way. It's an unhappy situation for everyone involved, isn't it?

Here are some suggestions for approaching someone about an annoying habit that could keep him or her from getting a job, a raise, or a promotion, or that could be even a serious handicap in establishing winning relationships.

To start with, be *tolerant.* You're human too, you know, and not perfect either. You should realize that we tend to be more critical of those we care for. Sadly, it seems like we're more tolerant of strangers than of those we love the most.

Evaluate the annoyance that the habit causes. Is it really that bad? Is it worth bringing up?

Remember that the chances are excellent the person might be unaware of his or her habit. A close friend of mine had the annoying habit of saying "huh?" to everything. I was able to help him by saying nothing, including not repeating what I had said. He soon broke the habit.

If you mention the habit, be sure to *attack the problem* and not the person. The problem is what you want to eliminate—not the person. Don't criticize unless you can offer a *solution.* Don't even mention it if you're not willing to invest some time in helping with the solution. Discuss the annoying habit gently, with love and concern for *helping* your friend.

Remember, a part of friendship is accepting a person in spite of his or her faults. But sometimes people need to be told. I believe if you'll follow these guidelines, you'll still have a friend after your conversation.

Action Steps

1. Today I will offer solutions rather than identifying problems.
2. Today I will_____

_____

No one is prevented by his own faults from pointing out those of another.
Latin Proverb

. . . Achieve

*W*here will you be when you get where you're going? In other words, where will your dreams take you? What are your ambitions and goals?

Perhaps you're like the salesman hopelessly lost who stopped at a general store in a rural community to ask for directions. The store owner winked at his friends and very convincingly replied, "You can't get there from here."

Is that the way you feel about your goals and dreams in life? Do you say to yourself, "I can't get there from here"? If you do, I can tell you that with an attitude like that you probably won't. Let me give you three suggestions that will help you reach your dreams in life.

Number one, don't be afraid to dream. Decide what you want in life. Scientific tests clearly prove that dreaming while you are asleep is critical to your emotional stability. Dreams while you are wide awake are just as important if you expect to realize more than a fraction of your potential.

Number two, identify the obstacles that stand between you and your goals and develop a plan to overcome those obstacles. Remember, if nothing stood between you and your desires you could simply claim them. As strange as it sounds, you will also have to decide if you're willing to enjoy the benefits that will come your way when you reach your goals.

Number three, don't be afraid to fail. Everyone encounters failures. It's how one deals with setbacks and disappointments that separates productive, fulfilled individuals from quitters.

Happy is the man who dreams dreams and is willing to take the steps to make them come true. Don't be afraid to start climbing and I'll see you at the top!

Action Steps

1. Today I will take time to think about where I want to be one year from today, and will analyze what I am doing to get there.
2. Today I will_____

_____

If people could only concentrate on their work as wholeheartedly as they concentrate on their worries, success would be assured.

. . . Give Yourself Away

*I*t only takes a few seconds to say a heartwarming thank-you. No American has lived a more hurried life than did Theodore Roosevelt, yet even on his busiest campaign treks, he always made time to stop and thank the engineer for a safe trip. It took only a couple of minutes of his time, and yet each time he made a friend for life. Good politics? Certainly! But good living, too.

In his delightful book, *Try Giving Yourself Away,* David Dunn offers a simple three-step formula to implement this strategy of gratitude. It came to him one morning as he approached a railroad crossing in New England.

> *Stop* as you rush through the day's activities.
> *Look* for opportunities to be courteous and friendly.
> *Listen* to others' hopes and problems so that you can contribute to their success and happiness.

By so doing, David Dunn concludes, "We'll find ourselves hugely enjoying life in spite of its troubles and uncertainties."

Remember to stop, look, and listen today and I'll see you at the top!

Thought: You can't smell the roses on the run. You have to stop to smell the roses, and you have to stop to enjoy life.

Action Steps

1. Today I will look for opportunities to be courteous, and I will seize those opportunities.
2. Today I will *listen,* with particular interest, to _____
   <small>(name)</small>

   _____ .

3. Today I will_____

   _____

Plenty of people miss their share of happiness, not because they never found it, but because they didn't stop to enjoy it.

William Feather

. . . Make Your Mark

I know you join me in wanting to make a mark on our world. One way you can be well on your way to doing just that is by seriously adopting Marshall Field's "ten guidelines for success." Incidentally, he was one of the most successful businessmen in the world, so his observations have considerable credibility.

1. The value of time—don't waste it.
2. The value of perseverance—don't give up.
3. The pleasure of hard work—don't be lazy.
4. The dignity of simplicity—don't be complicated.
5. The worth of character—don't be dishonest.
6. The power of kindness—don't be uncaring.
7. The call of duty—don't shun responsibility.
8. The wisdom of economy—don't be a spendthrift.
9. The virtue of patience—don't be impatient.
10. The improvement of skills—don't stop practicing.

I like these guidelines for success. They surprise many people because they are so plain and simple. Success is not complicated. Your actions are controlled by your thoughts and your thoughts are controlled by what you consistently inject or permit to be injected into your mind.

Action Steps

1. Today I will review the ten-step process for success as often as possible (at least ten times).
2. Today I will select one of the ten steps on which to concentrate, and one other for each of the next nine days. Today I will concentrate on step number _____ .
3. Today I will_____

_____

> *Some men succeed because they are destined to, but most men because they are determined to.*

162

. . . Alter Our Lives

*W*e've got some cleaning up to do and indications are strong it's going to be a big job. The astronauts of the space shuttle *Challenger* recently shared some alarming impressions of their trip in space. They said they saw a *dirty* earth. Paul Weitz, the commander of the first *Challenger* flight, said, "It was appalling to me to see how dirty our atmosphere is getting. Unfortunately, this world is becoming a gray planet. Our environment is flat going downhill. What's the message? We are fouling our own nest."

Now that's frightening news! Man is destroying his very home. It's time we did some cleaning up before it's too late. But there's another important area that also needs some special attention—effective immediately you can do something about it.

This area happens to be right between your ears. No, I'm not talking about your face. I'm talking about your mind and the pollution it absorbs. You're exposed every day to sex and violence on television and radio and possibly to profane language at work or school. The frightening danger is the way those negative stimuli affect your thoughts, attitudes, goals, and actions. How? We become what we think about and we think about what is put into our minds by ourselves or other people.

If you've got positive friends and positive information coming in, your life is guaranteed to be on the upswing. William James said, "The *greatest* discovery of my generation is that human beings can alter their lives by altering the attitudes of their minds." I hope you'll join me in cleaning up pollution of the mind, because if you do I'll see you at the top!

Action Steps

1. Today I will be conscious of *everything* that is going into my mind, and I will make every effort to put in only the good, clean, pure, powerful and positive.
2. Today I will_____

_____

An open mind leaves a chance for someone to drop a worthwhile thought into it.

. . . Influence Others

*Y*ou've heard it said a thousand times that example is the best teacher. Benjamin Franklin was one person who believed that old axiom. He felt that Philadelphia needed street lights, but knew that example would be more persuasive than argument. With this in mind, he devised a unique method of convincing his neighbors that Philadelphia should have those street lights. He hung a beautiful lantern on a long bracket outside his own door. He kept the lantern glass beautifully polished and the wick carefully trimmed.

Before long, Franklin's neighbors began placing lanterns outside their own doors. Soon the citizens of Philadelphia were ready to light their streets. Even Benjamin Franklin's most eloquent speeches were no match for the power or persuasiveness of his example.

That brings me to this question. How do you try to influence people? By intimidation? By steamrollering them into seeing your way? If so, you probably don't succeed too often. Even those times when you do, wreckage and hard feelings are probably left behind the successes.

I agree with Edgar A. Guest, who proclaimed, "I'd rather see a sermon than hear one any day." In short, doing and showing are more powerful than telling.

Action Steps

1. Today I will set the great example, remembering that *someone* (maybe even more than one someone) is studying and learning from me.
2. Today I will_____

The foundations of character are built not by lecture, but by bricks of good example, *laid day by day.*

Leo B. Blessing

. . . Speak

*H*ave you ever been called upon to give a speech—and the idea scared you to death? For some people, speaking in public is a frightening experience. No matter what your profession or job, there will be a time when you will be called upon to deliver a speech. It might be at an annual awards banquet, an office staff meeting, or maybe a monthly P.T.A. meeting.

Since public speaking can enhance your career opportunities, it's important that you at least learn the fundamentals. You don't have to be a professional speaker to give a good speech. You can, with a little practice, deliver a speech that is informative, interesting, and helpful to those who are listening.

Don't worry about being nervous. Remember that when an old mule is led in front of an audience it doesn't faze him a bit. Put a thorough-bred race horse in front of the same audience and he is as nervous as a long-tailed cat in a room full of rocking chairs! So if you are a little nervous when you speak before others, just thank God you are a race horse and not a mule.

Make eye contact with one smiling or friendly person at a time as often as possible. You'll probably be using some notes to keep yourself organized and on track, and that's fine, but do not read the speech.

Use words and phrases that are familiar to you. Make the speech from your own life or your own area of expertise. Be yourself. Don't try to sound fancy or base what you say on talk different from your everyday mode of speech. If you can't make a good speech while being truly yourself then you certainly can't make it by pretending to be someone else.

Finally, be enthusiastic. A speech is good when the speaker believes in and is enthusiastic about his message.

Action Steps

1. Today I will seize the opportunity to speak in front of a group (be it two or two hundred).
2. Today I will_____

_____

Fear is the sand in the machinery of life.

E. Stanley Jones

. . . Develop Friendship

*J*ack Benny and George Burns enjoyed a friendship that lasted fifty-five years. George Burns laughingly says, "He never walked out on me when I sang and I never walked out on him when he played his violin."

Dr. Alan McGinnis says there is a current shortage of friendships in our country. In his book, *The Friendship Factor,* Dr. McGinnis says that most folks don't have friendship on their priority list. But when you move from Seattle to Miami, you will be forced to develop new friends. How do you develop close friends?

One, *be honest.* Don't be afraid to be yourself. Cultivate some degree of openness in your life.

Two, *learn to forgive.* Remember that even friends make mistakes. If you need to clear the air, then do so, but don't pout or try to make your friend pay for what he did.

Three, *be thoughtful.* Learn the small but important gestures of friendship. Even though it doesn't seem like much when I send a card, it can really brighten my day if I receive a card from a friend. We assume our friends know how much they mean to us, but it doesn't hurt to remind them every now and then. Friendship is like every other area of life. It's something you must work at.

Thought: Seek understanding, not perfection, in a friend. After all, if the person was perfect, he might not want you for a friend!

Action Steps

1. Today I will make a friend by *being* a friend.
2. Today I will_____

_____

A friend is a present you give yourself.

Robert Louis Stevenson

. . . Win

*T*he date was May 28, 1983. The place: the French Open in Paris. Kathy Horvath, scheduled to play Martina Navratilova, had every reason to believe she'd lose. Martina was ranked number one in the world; Kathy was ranked forty-fifth. Although Kathy's record was good, it was not perfect. In contrast, Martina had not lost a match all year. In fact, she had won thirty-six straight matches! Her record in 1982 boasted ninety victories; the three defeats she experienced were to the likes of Chris Evert Lloyd and Pam Shriver. If all of these facts were not enough to upset Kathy's playing, there was more: they were playing in front of sixteen thousand and Kathy was only seventeen years old.

Kathy won the first set 6–4. Martina came back to win the second set 6–0. In the third set they battled to a 3–3 tie, with Martina serving. To everyone's surprise, Kathy Horvath won the set and the match. When asked about her strategy, the seventeen-year-old replied, "I was playing to win." I'm personally convinced that she won because she expected to win.

Expectancy is a great attitude. Evidence is conclusive that employer expectancy has a direct bearing on employee productivity and teacher expectancy has a direct bearing on pupil performance. Best of all, your personal expectancy has a direct bearing on your own performance. Plan to win, expect to win, believe you will win, and you will be a winner.

Action Steps

1. Today I will expect to win in all my activities.
2. Today I will_____

_____

The greatest pleasure in life is doing what people say you cannot do.
                                                          Walter Bagehot

---

. . . Get a Job

*L*ooking for a job? All of us have looked for a job at one time or another and know it can be a frightening and discouraging experience. There are many dos and don'ts when it comes to job hunting. However, if you will keep a few pointers in mind you may be very happily surprised to find that you can get the job you are looking for.

First of all, it's always good to have a brief résumé. Type up your work experience and have it ready for the prospective employer. Almost every employer wants to know something about the background of job applicants. Your résumé should be clear, honest, and simple—without gimmicks. State your past experience, with an emphasis on specific positive results that you were able to bring about for past employers.

Another tip to remember is to always dress your best. The first impression is very important, and even if you happen to be over-dressed for the job, the employer will know that you are sincere and eager to give a good appearance.

Most importantly, expect to get the job. Remember that now over one hundred million Americans are gainfully employed. In addition, since the overall average job turnover is about twenty percent each year, due to death, retirement, transfer, firings, resignations, and new job creation, this means that roughly 1.65 million new job openings are created every month. Surely you can get one of them!

Finally, be enthusiastic. Even if you don't have experience, almost every employer that I know is eager to have sincere and enthusiastic employees on the payroll.

Action Steps

1. Today I will work toward being a more productive individual by enthusiastically approaching my life.
2. Today I will_____

_____

There is no future in any job. The future lies in the man who holds the job.
Dr. George W. Crane

. . . Get a Cow out of the Cornfield

*H*ave you ever heard of the man named Artemus Ward? During the Civil War, humorist Artemus Ward boasted, "I have already given two cousins to the war, and I stand ready to sacrifice my wife's brother."

That line might rate a chuckle if it didn't strike so close to home. We all know people who are willing to go anywhere and do anything, as long as no effort, no expense, and no sacrifice is required. "Let George do it!" is the cry by everyone but George.

It's also easy to criticize others, blaming them for the mess you're in. Let me suggest, however, that a steady diet of criticism will lead to heartburn and maybe heart attack. Criticism seldom gets you anywhere—work does.

You can criticize a cow in the cornfield all day, and it will neither increase her milk production nor keep her out of the cornfield. Cows just aren't very receptive to criticism. However, you can lead the cow out and tie her to a stake or build a fence around the corn, and you've accomplished your objective. The difference between success and failure is often based on doing something about a problem instead of talking about it or wondering why no one else is doing anything.

Action Steps

1. Today I will take action on my ideas, instead of participating in lengthy discussions.
2. Today I will _____

_____

If you have something to do that is worthwhile doing, don't talk about it but do it. After you have done it, your friends and enemies will talk about it.

George W. Blount

... Deal with Stress

All of us face moments of stress and strain in our daily activities. According to the experts, a little stress is actually good, but too much stress and strain will cause you to lose sleep, make you edgy and irritable, and give you high blood pressure. Here are two ways to cut down on stress and keep yourself on an even keel.

First, deal with the cause of the stress. Is your primary problem today a misunderstanding with a co-worker or a family member? If so, take time to talk out the problem. It's best to swallow your pride, sum up your courage, and deal honestly with the conflict. Chances are excellent the problem is far less than you think—perhaps even a simple case of miscommunication. Nip that problem in the bud. If you let it build up in your mind, it causes unneeded and unwanted stress. The Bible says, "Don't let the sun go down on your anger," and that's good advice.

Two, find a pressure release. Take time to get away from it all for just a few moments each day. Perhaps some quiet reading, prayer or relaxation. Exercise like jogging, swimming, fast walking, or bicycling can work wonders in just a few minutes. You'll be amazed and delighted with the results.

I hope these tips will help you to cope with the tension that is a natural part of taking on a challenge and having a goal.

Action Steps

1. Today I will confront stressful situations immediately, rather than letting them grow.
2. Today I will take time for myself: to read, pray, meditate, exercise, or do whatever I need to do to unwind.
3. Today I will_____

_____

Take care of the minutes, for the hours will take care of themselves.
Lord Chesterfield

. . . Get a Promotion

*H*ave you ever wondered just what it takes to get promoted in your company? Employers look for certain characteristics in employees that mark them for promotion to management positions. Managing other people is not an easy task, so there are certain characteristics that every employer is looking for in prospective managers. Let's look at some important traits you can develop in your working relationships that will give you a better chance for promotion.

First is *forcefulness,* which is a trait you can and need to develop. You must develop the ability to skillfully make demands of others and increase their efforts. *Objectivity* is another important characteristic. You must learn to put your ego and emotions aside when discussing certain decisions. This is a difficult but obtainable goal. Of course, *self-discipline* is required. Good *organizational skills* and focused *concentration* despite all kinds of distractions are much-sought-after personality traits in any company.

Possibly the most important attitude you can develop is not caring who has the good idea. Your job as a manager will be to *give proper credit* to the creator of the idea and then to implement that idea for greater effectiveness.

Another important characteristic of the successful manager is the ability to surround yourself with people who have more talent and ability than you have. Management will pay more for *the ability to recognize and develop* talent than for any other ability. Add to these a touch of *compassion* and *true concern* for fellow workers, and your promotion is on the way.

Action Steps

1. Today I will copy the success traits from this list onto a three-by-five card to carry with me and review regularly.
2. Today I will_____

Doubt whom you will, but never doubt yourself.

Christian Bovee

172

. . . Learn More

One sure way to enhance your chances for success is to become a specialist in a particular field of knowledge or skill.

Every day new knowledge is made available to us through research in the ever-widening field of electronic media. This means that the sheer volume of information will make it increasingly difficult for one single individual to have all the facts in any field of business. Therefore, one way for you to become more helpful to your boss or manager is to become an expert in one particular area of importance. For example, you may work in real estate, where changes are so fast with regard to financing alone that it is impossible for one person to keep up with everything.

Pick out an area of interest to you that is of extreme importance to your company. Research it from every possible angle. Study trade journals, read books that are available, talk to recognized leaders in the field, and in general make yourself a valuable storehouse of information. Let your boss know what you are doing and offer to share your information with him. This helps him to look good and be more effective.

What you are really doing when you master a field and share information with your boss is making him more effective and making his job easier. Remember, you can get everything you want out of life if you will just help enough other people get what they want.

Action Steps

1. Today I will identify an area where I can help others by gaining additional knowledge—and I will begin to work to gain that knowledge.
2. Today I will_____

_____

It's what you learn after you know it all that counts.

. . . Imagine

*W*ould you be surprised to learn that you can practice your golf or tennis game for hours at a time and never move from your easy chair?

For years, Russian athletes have been winning more than their share of the gold medals in Olympic competition. American coaches have known about their intense training methods, but until recently we have been somewhat in the dark about the mental and psychological program that every Soviet athlete must endure.

At Stanford University, serious scientific study in the field of neuro-muscular behavior is taking place with the aid of sophisticated computers and the Stanford tennis team. Researchers have discovered a way for athletes to mentally practice arm and body movements while sitting in an easy chair.

I've been promoting the power of positive thinking for a long time and have solid evidence that you will perform exactly as you program your mind to perform. It's true of Olympic athletes and it is true of everyday behavior. You can code your mind so that you will *think* like a winner. Then you project on the screen of your mind the clear picture of yourself standing in the winner's circle receiving the award. These are the first and most important steps in becoming a winner.

Action Steps

1. Today I will picture exactly what winning means to me—physically, mentally, and spiritually—and I will focus on that mental picture.
2. Today I will_____

Man consists of body, mind, and imagination. His body is faulty, his mind is untrustworthy, but his imagination has made his life on this planet an intense practice of all the lovelier energies.

John Masefield

. . . Survive a Shaky Start

*I*f you are involved in your own business, don't be discouraged if you experience some rough times. Some of the most successful businesses in America knew shaky beginnings.

Most successful businesses do survive shaky starts. For example, Virginia Stone and Alma Mitchell sold two million dollars worth of stuffed animals last year, but just ten years ago they were thrilled to earn a few dollars per night selling door to door.

There are some common characteristics among small businesses that go on to make it big. First of all, they create products that have ready markets. Remember the old axiom: "Find a need and fill it." As times change and needs and desires change as well, there will always be opportunities for the creative entrepreneur in America.

Most successful businesses start out small and are operated by people who "throw away the clock" and work long hours until the business is "over the hump." Your best advice is to keep a limited budget and avoid overextending your cash flow. Finally, keep plugging away and be persistent in your pursuit of success with your business.

Action Steps

1. Today I will realize that even though someone else may sign my check, I determine the amount. I am in business for myself, marketing the products and services offered by me!
2. Today I will_____

_____

Wise men of today face the future unafraid.

Ernest C. Wilson

. . . Plan

After the American soldiers returned from World War II, there was a baby boom unmatched by any other period in history. G.I. Joe had had enough travel and hard times and was ready to settle down with a home and family.

Our schools were filled to capacity in the sixties and businesses which catered to that market reaped considerable profits. Now in the eighties, experts predict that the thirty-to-forty-four age group will be the most influential in the American marketplace. That age group will be growing three times as fast as it did over the past fifteen years. This means there will be a primary market for new homes, furniture, appliances, carpets, and household furnishings. The change in America's population structure means an incredible opportunity for those individuals tuned in to the needs of the market. A smart business person should slant much of his growth potential to that age group, and will always keep it in mind when making economic decisions.

Knowing your market, staying tuned in to the whims and needs of that market, and staying abreast of the latest products and trends which fit those market needs will put you one rung up on competition. A wise man once said that it was better to be at the right place at the right time than to be the smartest person in town. I believe that if you will properly plan and prepare for this mammoth market, you will be at the right place at the right time—and that just might make you the smartest person in town!

Action Steps

1. Today I will apply some long-range planning to my thoughts and ideas.
2. Today I will_____

_____

An intelligent plan is the first step to success.

. . . Overcome Fear

Success or failure can become a habit for all of us. Many people don't succeed because they have a fear of failure.

There is no question that many people never succeed because they are so afraid of failure they often don't make an effort to succeed. Fear of failure can be a serious problem. But let me give you some suggestions on how you might overcome your fear of failure so that you will be emotionally released to honestly try for success.

First of all, there are times when you have to simply force yourself to go ahead and try. Just suck it up, grit your teeth, and go ahead. For example, maybe you've been asked to make a speech but are scared to death. Well, it could be very rewarding to go ahead and make the speech through chattering teeth and shaking knees. (Incidentally, most people won't be able to see your chattering and shaking.)

Second, don't wait around until the situation is perfect before starting a project. Go ahead and start. Quit waiting for the perfect set of circumstances! If you wait until Aunt Matilda moves out, Charlie gets on the day shift, the new governor takes office, the new models are ready, or any other change in the facts outside of yourself before you make a commitment to go ahead and do something with your life, then, my friend, you will never do more than a fraction of what you are capable of doing.

Overcome fear of failure by starting out with small successes. Start with that first step. As the Chinese proverb reads, "A journey of a thousand leagues begins with but a single step."

Action Steps

1. Today I will overcome my fear by taking action on the things I fear.
2. Today I will_____

_____

Habits are at first cobwebs, and then cables.

. . . Win a Man to Your Cause

"*I*f you want to win a man to your cause, you must first convince him you are his friend," said Abraham Lincoln, one of the great persuaders of all time.

Yes, Abraham Lincoln was one of the great leaders of our country, and we remember him for many reasons. Chief among his many talents was his ability to win an argument. Perhaps we should say that it was the ability to persuade others to see his point of view. Persuasion was important for Lincoln's work as a lawyer, and it was important for his task of leading the nation.

Each of us must learn the skill of persuasion. It is a matter that has use every day. It might involve something as simple as trying to get your teenage boy to clean up his room (did I say simple?), or it may be that you are trying to make a big sale, the most important of your career. How can persuasion help?

Take a hint from Abe Lincoln. "If you want to win a man to your cause, you must first convince him you are his friend." The best way to do that is to be a sincere friend. Realistically, no one would ever try to persuade a friend to buy something or to take an action that was not in his best interest. Honest, sincere concern for the other man or woman is your most powerful ally in persuasion.

Action Steps

1. Today I will show my honest and sincere concern for those I meet.
2. Today I will_____

_____

Recipe for having friends: be one.

Elbert Hubbard

178

... Spend Wisely

*T*here is one asset we all have in the same quantity—at least at present.

I'd like to suggest a real picker-upper when you're feeling down in the dumps: spend something. No, I'm not talking about money. I suggest that you spend something that you have as much of as anyone else on a daily basis. I'm talking about time.

You can spend time in many ways, but I especially encourage you to spend it with someone who seldom has a chance to be with anyone: an invalid, a shut-in, a resident of an old folks home, or an elderly relative. This time could be a meaningful experience for you and a breath of fresh air for the person you visit. In addition, time spent with your family is always a good investment that will return many happiness dividends.

We are all given the same bank account every day of 1440 beautiful moments that we can invest wisely or squander wastefully. We can't store them, bank them, or save them. We've got to use them. Guard them jealously, use them wisely, and your life will be rewarding and exciting!

Action Steps

1. Today I will be aware of how I am spending my 1440 beautiful moments, and I will spend them wisely.
2. Today I will_____

_____

There is a loftier ambition than merely to stand high in the world. It is to stoop down and lift mankind a little higher.

Henry Van Dyke

. . . Move Ahead

*W*hen we get physically hungry, everyone knows we solve that problem by eating. Incredibly enough, most people do not know what to do when they get hungry emotionally, spiritually, or attitudinally.

The response to emotional, spiritual or attitudinal hunger is not quite as simple, nor is the solution always as fast, but it's just as definite as that for physical hunger. When you are down in any area of your life, I would like to assure you that there are written or otherwise recorded words that will provide the information and inspiration you need to get up. Whether your attitude is down and you are suffering from "stinkin' thinkin' " or whether you are spiritually or emotionally down, here is what you can do.

You can feed your mind and your emotions by deliberately seeking the company of inspiring people, by reading inspiring books on motivation, or by delving into good biographies or autobiographies. You can also listen to inspiring music or recordings. These things will change your attitude and feelings—and that means they will change your effectiveness and productivity. The message is clear. Change the input and you will change your output.

Action Steps

1. Today I will listen to or read at least one inspirational recording or piece of literature. I will then share the message with a friend.
2. Today I will_____

_____

A good listener is not only popular everywhere, but after a while he knows something.

Wilson Mizner

. . . Start Your Day

You can be number one!

I'm personally convinced that everybody can be number one. No, I don't believe that everyone can be the biggest, the fastest, the strongest, or the smartest, but I do believe you can be number one. Here's how.

Start each day of your life by looking in the mirror and saying, "Today I'm going to do my very best at whatever I do." Then proceed to do exactly that. At the end of the day, if you can again look yourself directly in the eye and say, "Today I did my best," you, my friend, will be number one with the most important person in the world as far as your success and happiness are concerned: *you!*

When you use what you have to the best of your ability, you will discover that your ability is more than adequate to reach your objectives. You will also discover that the more you use of what you have, the more you will be given to use.

Action Steps

1. Today I will start my day by looking into my eyes in the mirror and saying aloud: "Today I'm going to do my very best at whatever I do!"
2. Today I will_____

_____

"I can't do it" never yet accomplished anything; "I will try" has performed wonders.

George P. Burnham

. . . Appear Appealing

*O*ne problem with a partial truth, according to my friend, Dan Bellus, is that you often grab the wrong part!

Chances are excellent you have heard the expression, "You can't judge a book by its cover." Undoubtedly there is much truth in the statement. However, these six words, "Check your appearance, everyone else does," at least partially refute the "book-by-its-cover" cliché.

In everyday life, employers and prospective employers, as well as virtually every member of society, from bankers to teachers to members of the opposite sex, partially judge us by what they see. The old saying "You never get a second chance to make a good first impression," also has weight in this matter.

The message in this step to the top is simple. If you're looking for job advancement in your career, or a happier, more successful life, listen carefully to the truth in the old razor blade commercial popular a number of years ago: "Look sharp, feel sharp, be sharp!" Take that advice and I'll see you at the top!

Action Steps

1. Today I will be particularly aware and conscientious of the way I look and dress.
2. Today I will_____

_____

Of all the things you wear, your expression is the most important.

Janet Lane

. . . Be Understood

*M*any times in my presentations I use very simple examples. Then I explain to the audience that I speak and write at the seventh-grade, third-month level because I have discovered that even college professors can understand if I keep it very simple. Of course I am smiling, with my tongue firmly planted in my cheek.

I elaborate by pointing out that my good friend, Dr. Steve Franklin (a college professor from Emory University), often says, "Don't ever believe that the message has to be complicated to be effective. Words do not need four syllables to have meaning. Actually, there are only three colors, but look what Michelangelo did with those three colors! There are only seven notes, but look what Chopin, Beethoven, and Vivaldi did with those seven notes. For that matter, look at what Elvis did with two!" Generally speaking, the audience laughs at the humor, but the point is quite clear. Things can be beautiful without being complicated.

Eloquence is simplicity in motion. One of the most memorable speeches of all time is the Gettysburg Address. There are only 271 words involved, and 202 of them are one-syllable words.

I challenge you, in your life and in your communications, to let your thoughts run deep but to keep your expressions simple and direct. Whatever can be misunderstood will be misunderstood, and unnecessarily confusing ways of speaking will not help the matter. Simple, loving, direct communications will move more people into action and gain for you new friends, new insights, and greater happiness.

Action Steps

1. Today I will speak simply and directly and make no effort to overwhelm or impress anyone with my vocabulary.
2. Today I will_____

The average person's vocabulary is said to be about five hundred words. That's a small inventory, but think of the turnover.

. . . Visualize Success

I imagine most of us realize that self-confidence is an extremely important characteristic of every successful individual. The question to ask is, Where does self-confidence come from? Why are some people bubbling over with confidence, while others are frozen by a lack of trust in their abilities?

The fact is that self-confidence and success come in a cycle. Self-confidence comes from success, and it generates more success, which in turn generates more confidence. Now you might think from this explanation that the circle of success sounds like the ancient question about whether the chicken or the egg comes first. How do you break into the cycle?

The answer is simple: if you want more confidence in your life you must look to the small successes you have achieved and nurture the images and feelings that those victories have brought you. Forget the defeats and the failures that we all have. It's true that you want to learn from setbacks. But once you learn the lessons, forget the defeat and continue to think about, contemplate, and nurture the *victories* in your life. You will feed on those successes and your confidence will grow, allowing you to reach other greater successes.

Visualize your past victories while visualizing and anticipating future victories. Planting the seeds of positive expectancy in your mind is the best way to reap a positive harvest in the future.

Action Steps

1. Today I will make out a "victory list" of my ten best accomplishments over the past twelve months.
2. Today I will_____

Expect victory and you make victory.

Dr. Preston Bradley

. . . Listen

*A*ll of us like to talk, but sometimes we forget the most important part of a conversation. Most of us have spent at least a few moments trying to improve our speaking skills. It might have involved something as simple as the employee organizing his thoughts before he goes in to see the boss. Or it might have been like a young man arranging the words for his marriage proposal.

We believe that how we talk is very important, but we often forget that another aspect—our ability to listen—may be just as important. We are often guilty of thinking about our next sentence while another person is talking, rather than listening carefully to his or her exact words.

When you are in a conversation or a business negotiation, try to clear your mind of all your pet personal preferences and prejudices. Make an attempt to view the conversation in the clear light of day. Listen from the other person's frame of reference. What has he been through today? What is her general emotional state? Listen with your ears and your eyes. These factors will play an important role in how you view the actual words that are being said.

Good listening is a skill that requires practice, empathy, and true concern for the other person. The payoff is considerable, though, because good listeners traditionally learn a lot and have many, many friends.

Action Steps

1. Today I will listen with my heart and my ears to those I love most.
2. Today I will_____

_____

It is the province of knowledge to speak, and it is the privilege of wisdom to listen.

Oliver Wendell Holmes

. . . Create Instant Happiness

*W*hen anyone has the audacity to promise instant happiness, I suspect the chances are good that your first thought is, "Here comes somebody trying to sell me a false bill of goods!" I assure you, when I talk about immediately increased happiness, that's not my purpose.

My good friend Dr. Herb True, who is a fabulous speaker and is one of the funniest men around, says that if you would like to be instantly happier, you should try this exercise. Visualize losing every material possession you have, as well as being separated from every friend and relative you have. Hold that picture for a moment. Now visualize getting everything back.

You're far better off than you realized, aren't you? As you read these words, look around you. If you are in an office, on an airplane, riding in an automobile, or sitting in your home, you are probably surrounded by wealth that would stagger the imagination of millions of people on this earth.

As a practical matter, you do have a lot to be grateful for and happy about, don't you?

Action Steps

1. Today I will make a list of those things for which I am particularly grateful.
2. Today I will_____

_____

Remember, happiness doesn't depend upon who you are or what you have; it depends solely upon what you think.

Dale Carnegie

. . . Win Friends and Influence People

Many years ago, Dale Carnegie wrote a book entitled, *How to Win Friends and Influence People.* It has sold millions of copies and is the foundation for many Dale Carnegie courses. Personality development, which is one of the benefits of the course, is a sadly neglected skill in our country.

As a matter of curiosity, I would like for you to think about the people with whom you deal on a day-to-day basis. Almost without exception, the men and women who are happy and successful are pleasant, personable, and courteous.

I believe one of the most beneficial things we can teach our youth is simple, basic courtesy. I'll confess to being old-fashioned, but I believe that teaching the value of "please," "thank you," "yes, ma'am," or "yes, sir," is very important. I urge you to notice the number of executives and professionals who use words along those lines as a part of their regular vocabulary.

To go with common courtesy and respect, we should also throw in a good word about table manners. According to John Molloy, the author of *Dress for Success,* thirty percent of the job-seekers who are turned down for executive positions are turned down because of their table manners—actually, for the lack of them. Yes, courtesy and good manners are important if we are going to get to the top and stay there.

Action Steps

1. Today I will be particularly aware of the common courtesies. I will say "thank you" and "please" in a sincere and meaningful way.
2. Today I will_____

The wise man realizes that sincerity is the strongest force in the world and aligns himself with it.

Frank Crane

Love . . .

Where love is, there God is.

. . . and Goodness

*D*ean Cromwell coached at the University of Southern California for thirty-nine years. During that time, he produced twenty-one national championship winners, thirteen world record holders, and dozens of Olympic gold medalists. How? Dean Cromwell was an encourager. He was a "good finder" who emphasized a person's strengths.

One year in the Pacific Coast Track Championship, Cromwell's team needed to place in the final event, the mile relay. But Cromwell had four tired boys who earlier had lost in their individual performances. Only one was even a quarter-miler. He gathered the four around him in the middle of the track, determined to find something good, positive, and *true* he could say about each one. He told the first runner he was strong and could outrun anyone. He told the second, a hurdler, that a lap with no hurdles should make him the favorite. He told the third runner, a half-miler, that only a quarter mile should put him in the lead. He told the fourth runner, "You're the best on the track. Go out and show 'em you're a champ!" The team placed and won the championship.

Encouragement *is* stronger than criticism. The message of Dean Cromwell's success is clear. Be a "good finder," and before you know it, you will be surrounded by go-getters.

Action Steps

1. Today I will look for the good in others *and* will verbally compliment all those I can compliment sincerely.
2. Today I will be especially aware of looking for the good in _____ and will verbally compliment him or her as much as possible.
3. Today I will_____

_____

Look for strength in people, not weakness; good, not evil. Most of us find what we search for.

J. Wilbur Chapman

... and Friendship

*L*owell Davis of Savannah, Missouri, is eighty-three years old. If you've ever met him he knows, because he wrote your name down. A few years ago, Lowell wondered how many people he'd met in his lifetime. He bought a yellow binder, drew a big question mark on the cover and under it wrote, "How many people do you meet in a lifetime?"

Mr. Davis has written the names of everyone he has met—at least everyone he can remember—since he was three years old. In some cases he has written descriptions next to the name. For example, there's "Leonard McKnight—fond of chicken gravy." In Lowell Davis's case, he's met 3,487 people or sixty-nine pages worth, so far.

If my calculations are correct, Mr. Davis's records span 29,200 days since that third year of his life. He's met 3,487 people, or an average of one person every 8.37 days. Now think about it: If Mr. Davis believed you could get anything you want in life if you just helped enough other people get what they want, he would have had the opportunity to help 3,487 people reach their goals in life. If Mr. Davis had a goal of saying or doing something nice for someone every day, he would have performed over 29,000 good deeds! I recognize that the odds are good that Mr. Davis has not done something nice for everyone he's met. However, I firmly believe he has far more friends than ninety-nine percent of us, because his actions demonstrate a genuine interest in others.

Regardless of how old you are, you're in the people business. You're never too busy to say or do at least one nice thing for someone every day.

Action Steps

1. Today I will say or do something nice for _____
   _____ .

2. Today I will_____
   _____

Radiate friendship and it will be returned tenfold.

Henry P. Davidson

. . . and Sharing

More songs have been sung about, more verses have been recited concerning, and more hearts have been broken over one emotion, more than any other. The emotion is love. I, for one, think we've made love a little too mysterious. You see, I believe love is learned. Yes, learning to love is different from learning to ride a bicycle, but love *is* learned. And that's why some folks fail in love. They never learn how to love.

Now here's my suggestion. Don't save enjoyable times for special occasions. Work on sharing them daily. Let your loved one know that you enjoy every moment that you share, simply because you're spending it together.

Find activities that you both enjoy. For example, take a walk, play tennis, plant a garden, go sailing, or even wash your car. The important thing is that you share mutually enjoyable time together on a daily basis.

Of considerably more importance is the fact that you need to learn as much as you can about the object of your love. Real love reaches its zenith when two people are perfectly content just being together. That's why a reasonably long courtship is always advisable. If two people are happy and content just *being* together without *doing* anything, their chances of a happy marriage are much greater.

Love *can* be learned and continually improved. A positive attitude of growth in a love relationship might rekindle some dying embers, and it certainly can make life more enjoyable.

Action Steps

1. Today I will learn to love more by practicing on those closest to me.
2. Today I will_____

_____

The shared time of today is the beautiful meaning of tomorrow.

191

. . . and IOUs

*D*id you ever wonder what it would cost you to hire someone to serve as a night watchman, tutor, builder, architect, and nurse? Chances are excellent this person already works for you. The multi-talented person's identity? Your mother. I'd like to share a beautiful tribute by Marjorie Cooney.

"I've been thinking, Mother. For a long time now, I've carried some IOUs around with me. It's high time I paid up, Mom. I owe you for night watchman services. The nights you got little sleep because of real or imagined noises, the nights you stayed up doctoring us, the nights you didn't count sheep but talked with the Good Shepherd.

"There's a huge IOU here for construction work. You didn't know you were an architect and builder, did you? You worked hard to build our hopes and dreams, our confidence. You exhausted yourself cementing your family together with the glue of love and fidelity. You hammered into us dependability, reliability, and just about every ability it takes in life to get along with others in a wholesome, meaningful way. My IOU for teaching services is beyond my ability to pay. Most of what I've learned of life, I learned at your knee.

"Yes, the payment of these IOUs is long overdue. My debt to you is awesome. But I know you'd mark the whole bill 'paid in full' for a kiss and those four little words which are priceless: 'Mother, I love you!' "

Action Steps

1. Today I will pay back some of my IOUs.
2. Today I will_____

_____

If you have not often felt the joy of doing a kind act, you have neglected much—and most of all yourself.

A. Nielsen

. . . Poverty

I'm going to talk about a poverty which has nothing to do with money. Normally when someone mentions poverty, we think of those people who do not have enough money to buy the things necessary to sustain life at a tolerable level. But there is another type of poverty we need to become acquainted with in order to avoid: *relational poverty*.

People who can't get along with others, who have no close friends or family with whom they can effectively and pleasantly deal on a daily basis, are impoverished socially. How tragic it is for someone to go through life not getting to know and share some of the innermost feelings, joys, and sorrows of friends, peers, and fellow human beings.

We know about the form of poverty that is concerned with lack of money; what about more subtle forms? One is to think poorly of ourselves. Yet another is to cheat ourselves of time with our children. Still another is to hoard throughout our lives our potential laughs and fun without cashing them in.

Realize first your own value, then the value of others. Now combine those values and watch the growth, feel the excitement in the new bond of joy, and realize the stability of having set up a "people trust fund" to guard against *relational poverty*.

Action Steps

1. Today I will make a large deposit in my "people trust fund" by listening carefully to, complimenting freely, and believing sincerely in people.
2. Today I will_____

_____

If you wish to be loved, first you must love!

193

. . . and Humility

*A*ll of us are a pain to live with when we're wrong—and we may even be when we're right! This is probably the reason chaplain Peter Marshall prayed, "Lord, when we're wrong make us willing to change, and when we're right make us easy to live with." That touches a sensitive nerve, doesn't it? It's hard to resist strutting when we've been proven right.

Parents teach children how to be good losers because they know that the kids will sometimes lose, and they need to learn how. But I think we parents often fail to teach them another important lesson—how to win, how to be gracious winners. Is it because we're not sure how to win gracefully ourselves?

Humility is a much-desired characteristic. It should be fairly easy to acquire, because most of us have a lot to be humble about. No one comes into this world by himself, and no one succeeds or even survives by himself. A truly humble person realizes even in successful times that he owes a debt to many others. Additionally, he will not leave this world as a very lonely person, because he will have learned the value of others. I encourage you (as I encourage myself) to practice daily being easier to live with.

Action Steps

1. Today I will remember to "share the wealth" by giving credit to others who participate in my successes.
2. Today I will thank God for my successes, for it truly is by his grace that all things come to me.
3. Today I will_____

_____

There is no limit to what can be accomplished when no one cares who gets the credit.

John Wooden

. . . and Toughness

*W*ant to reduce delinquency? Then teach them how to read.

Dr. Alice Blair, superintendent of Chicago's District 13, points out that ninety percent of all teenage male delinquents read below the third grade level. She believes that delinquency is a cry for self-esteem. Students who cannot read have difficulty believing in themselves.

In 1971, Dr. Blair took over as principal of the George Maniere Elementary School in Chicago, a school where pre-teens gambled in the hallways, sipped wine in the rest rooms, and threw chairs through the windows. At the time she took charge only three students out of an enrollment of eight hundred read at grade level. After three years with Dr. Blair, fifty percent of the Maniere students were reading at grade level or above.

Her philosophy is expressed by a sign on her desk, "If God had approved permissiveness, He would have given us the 'Ten Suggestions.' " Dr. Blair is a mixture of the tough task-master and the understanding mother. Tough children respect her and the little ones enjoy her warm hugs. This approach gets results.

Do you love enough to do what is best for those for whom you care? If you will keep hugging without compromising right and wrong, then those you love will respect you *and* benefit personally.

Action Steps

1. Today I will speak positively of others and will walk away from negative conversations.
2. Today I will_____

_____

Permissiveness is simply neglect of duty.

. . . and Appreciation

*T*ennessee Congressman Ed Jones tells about the woman from the city who didn't appreciate the time he was spending on the agriculture committee. "What do we care about agriculture?" she fumed. "We get all *our* groceries at the supermarket!"

That remark wouldn't make sense even to the person who said it if she were not so consumed by her own concerns. But then again, we all see our own problems as more important than the problems of others.

We depend on others. Think about that egg you enjoyed for breakfast. A store sold it, a truck delivered it, a farmer packed it, and a hen laid it. Along the way many people were involved. The grain which fed the hen was raised by another farmer who bought his farm equipment from manufacturers who employed dozens of workers. The truck which delivered the egg was fueled with gasoline that had been refined and delivered by other workers. Tracing this tree of dependence could go on indefinitely, but I think you get the idea.

We're indebted to many people. Our parents, our teachers, our friends, our spouses—and the list continues. Not one of us lives alone and apart. As the marvels of our age multiply, each person's influence expands, but so does his dependence. Just think about your groceries.

Action Steps

1. Today I will be more appreciative of those around me and express my appreciation with *sincere* thank-yous as often as possible.
2. Today I will be particularly sure to remind _____
   _____ how much I appreciate him or her.
3. Today I will _____

   _____

Appreciation of what we have is at least half of the true way of life.

. . . and Youth

Does this sound like a familiar statement: "Children no longer obey their parents and they gobble up their food!"? Sounds serious, doesn't it? There are people today who have a very negative view toward our youth. But before we go any further let me say that that statement was written over four thousand years ago somewhere in the Nile Valley.

From the beginning, there have always been people who thought their generation was the worst or the meanest of all time. And there are people today who believe that we as a country don't have a future. I'll admit there was a time during the sixties and early seventies when I suffered from a small case of that "stinkin' thinkin'." I was beginning to wonder if we hadn't lost our bearings and were on a downhill treadmill.

Fortunately, the pendulum is now making a swing back to a more sane and solid approach to living. When parents start teaching respect and discipline, with lots of love thrown in, our young people will really be prepared for productive careers. I believe today's youngsters are bright and sharp and deserve the advantage of being taught discipline and responsibility. That's the only way they can grow and be prepared to accept the reins of business and government so they can leave bright futures for the generation that follows them.

Action Steps

1. Today I will look for the good in the youth with whom I come in contact, and will give them a positive advantage by sharing ideas of discipline and responsibility.
2. Today I will_____

_____

The youth of a Nation are the trustees of Posterity.

Benjamin Disraeli

. . . and Kindness

*A*n act of kindness and compassion saved Dr. Pinel's life. Here's the story.

It was eighteenth-century Paris. A man named Chevigne was headed for prison, though he had committed no crime. Just weeks before, his mind had broken; he was now being taunted by the crowd that watched his sad journey. The prison wagon passed an apartment window where a physician named Phillipe Pinel saw him. Dr. Pinel was overwhelmed by the utter despair in Chevigne's eyes.

Years later, Pinel won the undying gratitude of the mentally ill when he became a pioneer in humane treatment for those suffering that malady. Eventually, he headed the hospital to which Chevigne had been taken. When Dr. Pinel found Chevigne in a dungeon, he ordered him released.

Over the years protests from the medical community arose against Pinel's new measures of treatment. On one occasion Dr. Pinel was literally mobbed. Out of the crowd came a man who carried Pinel to safety. The grateful doctor stated, "I owe you my life." The man smiled in response. "Two years ago I was chained in a dungeon. You set me free. My name is Chevigne." There's that bread cast upon the waters, isn't it?

When you do something for someone who cannot immediately return the favor, this is truly an act of love. If you will do what you know is right, in an attitude of love, good things will happen for you!

Action Steps

1. Today I will act with kindness and compassion toward all I meet.
2. Today I will_____

_____

Kindness consists of loving people more than they deserve.

. . . and Discipline

*T*he parent who won't discipline his child might do so because of a poor self-image. In the family, a poor self-image is often manifested by parental reluctance to discipline the child. The parent hides this under the mask of permissiveness: "I love him so much I can't deny him anything."

Actually, the parent is often fearful of causing the child to withdraw or withhold his or her love. The unfortunate truth is that this often causes the parent to lose control and even lose respect and love. The child loses confidence in the parent and the security that goes with knowing who is in charge. Soon the child's self-image is damaged too, with ever-widening consequences.

This is the first step in the loss of respect for authority that ultimately leads to rebellion against authority. The tragedy is that many problems could be averted if parents and teachers knew how to recognize the signs of a poor self-image. The child's actions so clearly say "notice me," "love me," "I want you to care what I do!"

Parents and teachers, when you discipline that child, you're saying to the child that you care so much about what he does that you're going to exert an influence to direct what he does.

Action Steps

1. Today I will love all those around me enough to say what they need to hear.
2. Today I will_____

_____

The parent who loves the child will do what needs *to be done, not what the child* wants *to be done.*

... and Hate

*R*ev. Rudy Baker of the St. John's Methodist Church in Augusta, Georgia, tells the story of a lady whose doctor saw her furiously writing after she was bitten by a mad dog. The doctor gently assured her that there was no need to make her will, that she was going to be all right, they were going to give her a shot that would take care of the disease. The lady looked at the doctor and said, "I'm not worried about dying. I'm making a list of all the people I'm going to bite before you give me that shot!"

Well, I don't know if the story was fact or fiction, but I do know that when we carry hate for other people it is totally self-defeating. Psychologically, the Bible is right on target when it tells you to forgive your enemies and to ask them to forgive you. You probably are at least partially wrong, and when you clean the deck with them you also clean the deck with yourself. When your mind is free and clear of hate, you can do much better in anything that you have to do.

Action Steps

1. Today I will free my mind of hate by forgiving and asking forgiveness of a person with whom I have had a dispute. That person is
   _____ .

2. Today I will_____

   _____

It is difficult to live in the present, ridiculous to live in the future, and impossible to live in the past.

Jim Bishop

. . . and Encouragement

Can a shout and a yell score a touchdown or sink a free throw? It is an established fact that the home court or home field gives competing athletic teams a definite advantage. The cheerleaders and the general public might not even know the difference between a first down and a touchdown, but they know when their guys do something good. They can be counted on to yell and stomp their feet to encourage their team. Coaches and players alike repeatedly say that the support of the local fans pulling for them, encouraging them, and cheering them on is an advantage worth several points to the home team.

What a shame that we don't realize—and capitalize on—the encouragement factor in our everyday lives. Husbands and wives should pull and cheer for each other, parents should encourage and cheer for their children, and kids in turn should cheer for their parents. Ditto for employees and employers.

This approach would make for more productive business, which would mean more money for everyone and better service for the customers. The message is clear and simple. If all of us cheered for and encouraged our friends, relatives, and associates, America would be an even better place to live and work!

Action Steps

1. Today I will cheer for and encourage _____
   _____ .

2. Today I will _____
   _____

Wherever there is a human being there is an opportunity for kindness.

. . . and Impressing Others

An attractive lady was taken to dinner by William Gladstone, the distinguished British statesman. The next evening she attended a dinner where she sat next to Benjamin Disraeli, his equally distinguished opponent.

Later, when someone asked her opinion of the two men, she replied, "After sitting with Mr. Gladstone I was convinced he was the cleverest man in England. But after sitting next to Mr. Disraeli, I thought I was the cleverest woman in England!"

The example is intriguing because there is so much common sense and truth in it. If you want to persuade people and win them to your way of thinking, the best way to do so is to talk in terms of their interests. Give them the feeling that they have value as persons, that they can do the job, that they have potential and ability.

If you are sincere, others will come to the conclusion that you are an all-right person.

Action Steps

1. Today I will satisfy in others what some have called "the greatest human need," the need to feel important. I will satisfy this by showing a sincere interest in each individual with whom I come into contact.
2. Today I will_____
   _____

Selfishness with much can do little, but love with little can do more.

202

. . . and Helping Others

*W*hen Sir Edmund Hillary and his native guide, Ten Sing, made the historic climb of Mount Everest, Sir Edmund became the first man in history to reach the peak. While coming down the mountain, Sir Edmund lost his footing, but Ten Sing held the line taut and kept them both from falling by digging his axe into the ice.

Ten Sing refused any special credit for saving Hillary's life. He considered it a routine part of the job and expressed it simply but eloquently when he said, "Mountain climbers *always* help each other."

What a fantastic philosophy! How unfortunate that this philosophy is not adopted by literally everyone in our country. How much better off we would be. Maybe everyone won't adopt this standard, but since you just read this message, you can adopt it. That means you'll be better off and so will the people you influence. If enough people hear this healthy philosophy and spread the word, we will have an even better America.

Action Steps

1. Today I will remember that human beings always help each other. I will reach out and look for opportunities to help others.
2. Today I will_____

_____

Duty makes us do things well, but love makes us do them beautifully.

. . . and Children

*J*odie will go anywhere in the world to get a kid.

Jodie (Mrs. Dick) Darragh is a smart, pretty, compassionate, and energetic homemaker. She and her sales rep husband live in a typical middle-class house with middle-class mortgage, taxes, car repairs, and the cavities of three kids.

But from the kitchen counter of their modest home in Marietta, Georgia, they run an international volunteer agency called Americans For International Aid. They've rescued thousands of kids from death, disease, and hunger. How do they do it? Love, desire, and hard work. They *want* to rescue kids in Vietnam, Columbia, India, Korea, and other trouble spots in the world.

Every day, by phone, letter, or visit, Jodie brings together hundreds of volunteer flight attendants who pick up and deliver kids, dozens of adoption agencies and relief missions, and hundreds of American families who want to adopt.

Walk into Jodie's home and the phone will probably be ringing, carrying tears, laughter, or pleas. It might be Ted Koppel of ABC's "Nightline" requesting an interview. It might be Senator Jeremiah Denton requesting information on the Amerasian bill. It might be one of a hundred expectant fathers or mothers asking, "Did the plane leave yet? Do you think she'll get here today?" And Jodie's answer is always, "Sit back, drink a cup of coffee, and relax. Your kid's coming home."

Jodie and Dick don't get paid. And twenty percent of Dick's hard-earned salary gets plowed into the work of Americans For International Aid. "It's God's work," says Jodie. "God's gotta be in this thing, or it'd never fly."

Like Jodie and her husband, if you will give what you have, when you can, then I truly will see you at the top!

Action Steps

1. Today I will seek to help those who need help.
2. Today I will_____

_____

> *Then the righteous will answer him, 'Lord, when did we see thee hungry and feed thee, or thirsty and give thee drink? And see thee a stranger and welcome thee or naked and clothe thee?'... And the King will answer them: 'Truly, I say to you, as you did it to one of the least of these, you did it unto Me.'*
>
> Matthew 25:37–40

. . . and Marriage

*C*ouples who pray together, stay together. Couples who worship, stay wedded. Unfortunately, the last time some couples were in church was on their wedding day. And they wonder why, four and a half years later, they are dickering with a lawyer over a divorce settlement.

What does going to church do for a marriage? First, it prevents breakdown. Going to church together is like taking your car to the original service department. The folks who built the car know best how to keep it in top shape. The one who created marriage knows best how to keep it in top shape. His "service manual" is the Bible and his "fix-it" shop is the church.

Second, you associate with folks who value marriage as you do. A leading magazine headlined: "You Can *Too* Steal Her Husband!" A leading film advertised, "First, the good news. The good news is that Charlie is having his first affair. The bad news is that it's with his roommate's mother."

Why is it "good news" that someone is having an affair? Why urge another to steal someone's mate? What's a good way to protect yourself from this attack on marriage? Be around folks who cherish marriage as highly as you do.

Third, church reminds us of the commitment of love. Jesus talked about the highest form of love: "Greater love hath no man than this, that a man lay down his life for his friends" (John 5:13). In church, through sermons and Bible classes, we are reminded that "laying down one's life" also includes the very practical sacrifices of putting a mate's feelings and interests before one's own. We see our Christian friends doing it and it encourages us to do the same. In church, we get public reminders and public examples of the beauty of love.

It's interesting, but the first place that people run to when they're desperate and hurting is church. Deep down, everyone knows that love is where church is. Want to keep marriage alive and well? Put God in the center.

Action Steps

1. Today I will pay particular attention to my spouse by saying something nice *to* him or her and by saying something nice *about* him or her.
2. Today I will_____
   _____

Husbands, love your wives, even as Christ loved the church and gave Himself for her.

Ephesians 5:22

. . . and the Scrap Heap

I know of a blacksmith who placed a sign above his shop hearth saying, "The Fire, Lord, not the Scrap Heap."

The meaning? "Well, sir," says the blacksmith, "I shove my horseshoes right in here—the hotter the coals the better. After awhile, I pull a shoe out and put it on my anvil. I beat it and hit it to see if the iron in the shoe is hard and tough. If it is, I shove it back in the fire and make it into a finished shoe. If it bends or cracks 'cause it ain't tough, I throw it into that scrap heap with the other pieces of junk." The Fire, Lord, not the Scrap Heap.

God says: "Do not be surprised at the fiery trials that come upon you to prove you, as though something strange were happening to you" (1 Peter 4:12). God allows trials of fire to make us tough. People without trials are about as useful as scrap on a heap of junk. God allows problems to make us tough. God allows problems to build us up.

No one enjoys the variety of problems which hit us: job loss, no calls for dates, heartbreak in the home, betrayal by a friend, death of a loved one. No one goes looking for problems. But when God allows problems, we look for God's purposes *in* those problems.

We know that God allows problems, not to stop us but to start us. God never stops people—God only starts people.

Action Steps

1. Today I will seek the purpose behind "opportunities"—what some folks might call "problems"—that arise for me.
2. Today I will_____
   _____

All things work together for good to those that love God and are called according to His purpose.

Romans 8:28

208

. . . and Prayer

*P*eople who believe in God have no problem praying for others, but are sometimes embarrassed to pray for themselves. Is it okay for one to pray for oneself? Absolutely!

The Bible gives four examples. In Luke 18:1–7, the story is told of a woman who returns again and again to a judge to plead her rights. Reluctant at first, the judge finally gives in and gives the woman what she wants. Jesus commends the woman, urging his disciples to "never give up and never be discouraged in praying." God is our Father. We know that our own earthly fathers love to give to us. We know that they love for us to go to them to talk about our requests.

In Matthew 7:7 (part of the Sermon on the Mount), Jesus says, "Ask, and it will be given you; seek, and you will find; knock, and it will be opened to you." Know what you want and ask God for it. A great hindrance to prayer is not in God—it is in the person praying. Write down what you want and talk to God about it. If it is proper and good, he will open the door and provide it.

Matthew 26:39 records Jesus' agony in the Garden of Gethsemane. He prayed for himself in the garden, asking, "If it be possible, let this cup pass from me." Notice that he added the important request, "Not as I will, but as You will."

In the Lord's Prayer or model prayer, Jesus tells us to make the specific request: "Give us this day our daily bread." Put before God your needs. He's your Father. He'd love to hear from you!

Action Steps

1. Today I will list my needs on paper and pray to God to help me meet these needs, understanding that they will be met in God's way on his timetable, and not mine.
2. Today I will_____

_____

Trust in the Lord with all your heart, and do not rely on your own insight. In all your ways acknowledge Him, and He will direct your paths.

Proverbs 3:5,6

. . . and Wealth

*I*n Matthew 19:24–26, Jesus said: " 'It is easier for a camel to go through the eye of a needle than for a rich man to enter the Kingdom of Heaven.' When his disciples heard it, they were exceedingly amazed, saying, 'Who then can be saved?' But Jesus beheld them, and said unto them, 'With men this is impossible; but with God all things are possible.' "

Now some interpret the "needle" in this passage to refer to a small opening at the base of the wall in Old Jerusalem. Presumably, a camel got down on his knees and *squeezed* through. In other words, it's a difficult squeeze, but it *is* possible. That's not the point of this story, if we hear what the disciples said. Jesus refers to a *real* camel going through the eye of a *real* needle.

And that is *impossible!* This is the point of the story. It is impossible for a camel to go through the eye of a needle, and it is impossible for any person (rich or poor) to save himself. If a camel is to go through the eye of a needle, God will have to cause it to happen. If a person is to be saved, God will have to do it for him. That is exactly what God, in Christ, did for us.

You see, a lot of people are miserable because they are trying to get right with God on their own. They think they get right by going to church, giving money, or doing good deeds. But remember, no matter what a camel does, there is no way he can go through the eye of a needle. Something supernatural has to happen. It has to be miraculous. That is the way it is with our relationship with God. Something miraculous had to happen. Something miraculous did happen—and it happened for you!

Action Steps

1. Today I will "let go and let God."
2. Today I will_____

For God so loved the world that He gave His only begotten Son, that whosoever believeth in Him should not perish, but have everlasting life.

John 3:16

. . . and Ability

Dr. Norman Vincent Peale tells the story of visiting a poor family, and the interesting exchange they had. "The husband, Bill, dolefully recounted their miseries. But the wife carried on a sprightly conversation, saying, 'God will show us the way.'

"I noticed that she was working on a bright piece of material that looked like a mitten and I asked her what it was. 'Oh, it is just a potholder dressed up,' she replied. Then an idea popped into my mind, put there by God, answering the woman's faith. 'Why don't you send Bill down to the department store?' I suggested. 'I think they would buy them. At least it's worth trying.'

"Bill went down to the buyer and to his surprise got an order for a gross of them. That simple thing started a new business which ultimately employed quite a few people.

"'Funny,' said Bill, 'how God answers prayers through potholders.'

What did Bill's wife have in her hand? A potholder. And God used it to lift a family from poverty and despair. What do you have in your hand? That was the question God asked Moses. Moses said, "A stick." God said, "I'll use that stick in your hand to do powerful things and free the children of Israel."

What do *you* have in *your* hand? That's the question God asks you. Oh, I know what some folks say. "If I had the money Rockefeller has, or the voice of Roberta Peters, or the brain of Einstein, what wouldn't I do for the Lord?" The answer to that fantasy is not a cotton-pickin' thing! If you're not using what you have, you won't use what you don't have!

What is that in your hand now, that you can use right now?

Action Steps

1. Today I will use my abilities as God would have me use them.
2. Today I will _____

Save time thinking you can do the other fellow's job better than he can—put it into doing your own job better!

H. A. Schenfeld

. . . and Thankfulness

*I*n an article I recently read, my friend Neil Gallagher, an outstanding author, wrote about thankfulness. Let's listen in.

Today, I thank God that:

I can see
—the splash of a rainbow
—the lattice of a snow flake
—the gold of the sun
—the purple pink of dusk

I can smell
—fresh fish
—just-cut lemons
—newly-mowed hay
—talcum-powdered babies

I can hear
—semi-trailers blaring on highways
—the ring of a phone
—hot jazz and cool blues
—the whispered secret of a grandson

I can feel
—the embrace of my mate against me
—the sharp of cold and the sting of pain
—my heart beating and eyes blinking
—the veins of a leaf

I can taste
—the bite of hot-sauce on an unsuspecting tongue
—the crunch of chips and the smooth of yogurt
—the tang of just-sliced grapefruit
—the mellow of spiced tea

Today, I give thanks for eyes, nose, ears, touch, and tongue— avenues to know the good of the world and the goodness of God.

Today, I give thanks for family and friends, my faith and my flag.

Today, I give thanks for all.

Today, I say: "Lord, You have given me so much. Give me one more thing—a grateful heart."

Isn't that a beautiful thought? Thank you, Neil, for the beautiful words that communicate so clearly.

Action Steps

1. Today I will spend the day with gratitude in my heart for the "little things" of life.
2. Today I will _____

_____

Giving thanks always and for all things.

Ephesians 5:20

. . . and Prevention

*H*ave you ever noticed that most of your friends accept your good behavior without much fanfare or comment? But the moment you do something wrong you are immediately hit with reminders, reprimands, and sometimes something much worse.

I'm sure you have noticed that about those around you, but have you ever stopped to realize that you may be guilty of the same thing? Perhaps you are guilty of taking the good behavior of your friends, spouse, or children for granted. Maybe you haven't appreciated the fact that your children are doing well in school, are responsible and safe drivers, and have friends who are solid young citizens. Sometimes we forget the good points and respond only to the negative.

Let me urge you to try a little "preventive loving." Encourage your children today by complimenting them for the areas in their lives where they are doing well. Practice preventive loving within your own family, and make a habit of praising friends, fellow workers, and acquaintances.

If you will use preventive loving, you will foster those characteristics in others that will help them to be winners, and by helping them to be winners, you will be a winner too!

Action Steps

1. Today I will practice preventive loving by encouraging _____ _____ and _____ .
2. Today I will _____
   _____

As a neglected garden is soon invaded by weeds, so a love carelessly guarded is quickly submerged by unkind feelings.

Andre Maurois

Perseverance . . .

Fight one more round. When your feet are so tired that you have to shuffle back to the center of the ring, fight one more round. When your arms are so tired that you can hardly lift your hands to come on guard, fight one more round. When your nose is bleeding and your eyes are black and you are so tired that you wish your opponent would crack you one on the jaw and put you to sleep, fight one more round—remembering that the man who always fights one more round is never whipped.

James J. Corbett

. . . and Concentration

*T*homas Edison accomplished more in his lifetime than ten average men do. His contribution to modern society is almost impossible to measure. He invented the phonograph, the electric locomotive, the microphone, a method for constructing concrete buildings, a device for producing sheet metal, a telegraph signal box, and of course, the incandescent electric lamp.

What is the quality in one individual that enables him to make such a mammoth contribution to society? Is it genius? Is it opportunity? Is it fate?

We may never know all the answers to these questions, but we do know something about the work of Thomas Edison. He worked long hours. He had the ability to concentrate, to focus all of his mind, body, and soul on one particular project until it was completed to his satisfaction. The ability to concentrate was an essential ingredient in the success of Thomas Edison. When he was working on a project he put the blinders on and concentrated solely on that project. He developed tunnel vision and permitted no distractions. His persistence was legendary. He performed over ten thousand experiments before he produced the first incandescent light.

What about you and your projects? Do you have goals that you are able to put your whole mind, body, and spirit into?

Action Steps

1. Today I will identify the five most important tasks to my success, put on the blinders, and work with intensity until I am satisfied with the work.
2. Today I will_____

_____

Work does more than get us our living; it gets us our life.

Henry Ford

. . . and Hope

*F*or eight years he wrote short stories and articles for publication, and for eight long years they came back as rejections. He didn't give up, though, and for that we will always be grateful.

While he was in the Navy he wrote a mountain of routine reports and letters. After his hitch in the Navy was over he tried desperately to make it as a writer. For eight long years he sent stories and articles off to magazines but was never able to sell even one. On one occasion an editor wrote an encouraging note on the form rejection slip; it said simply, "Nice try." The young writer was moved to tears and given new hope.

He was not the kind of man to give up. Finally, after many years of effort he wrote a book that deeply affected the entire world. He titled it *Roots*. Yes, Alex Haley, after years of diligent application, finally saw his efforts rewarded as he became one of the most successful and influential writers of the seventies.

Be persistent, be hopeful, and work hard toward your dream. Persistence, dedication, hope, and hard work might not sound very glamorous, but they are the ingredients necessary to take you out of mediocrity and make your dreams come true.

Action Steps

1. Today I will be persistent and hopeful and will work hard, and in my tomorrows I will reap the rewards of what I sow today.
2. Today I will_____

_____

> *To get through the hardest journey we need take only one step at a time, but we must keep on stepping.*

. . . and Work

*H*ow would you like to leave your homeland, leave family and friends, and move to another country to start all over? That is exactly what Carlos Arboleya did over twenty years ago, after Castro took over the banks of Cuba.

In 1960 Carlos had worked his way up the ladder to a position as an accounts officer in one of the largest banks in Cuba. But one morning he came to work to discover that all private banks had been taken over by Castro's communist regime. Three weeks later Carlos was able to get himself, his wife, and his small son out of Cuba to freedom in America.

He had forty-two dollars. He did not have a job, nor did he know a single person in his new country. He went to every bank in Miami but had no luck finding work. He finally found a job in a shoe factory taking inventory. He worked so tirelessly that within sixteen months he was the manager of the shoe company. In a short time he was offered a job in the bank where the shoe company did its banking. The rest is history. Carlos Arboleya is one of the most successful bankers in America today.

From inventory clerk at a shoe factory to president of the largest chain of banks in Miami—that is the story of one positive refugee. Where you start isn't important. Where you end up is important.

Action Steps

1. Today I will start where I am, with what I have, and begin my journey to success.
2. Today I will_____

_____

Little and often make much.

. . . and Determination

*P*atricia Slagle was fifty years old and looking for work five years ago. Now she's enjoying a six-figure income.

Patricia Slagle had spent her entire adult life in Syracuse, New York, mothering four sons and occasionally giving piano lessons. When her marriage broke up she spent six years earning little money in various jobs.

A friend suggested she try the world of finance, but most brokerage firms weren't interested in a fifty-year-old rookie. During the interviews, Patricia remembers, "I walked in and swallowed hard, pretending confidence I certainly did not feel." Finally, her persistence paid off; Merrill Lynch hired Pat as a stockbroker.

The move to a new community in a new profession was difficult, but the motivation was compelling—Pat needed the money. Success in her new field didn't come easily, but the persistence and determination that won her the opportunity in the first place provided her with the fuel to make the most of that opportunity. Today, at age fifty-six, Patricia Slagle earns a six-figure income—due to hard work and the courage to try.

Thought: You never know what you can do until you give it a try.
Question: Don't you really believe you owe yourself that chance?

Action Steps

1. Today I will work diligently and not be afraid to make the effort— and extra effort—that will mean success.
2. Today I will_____

Keep trying. It's only from the valley that the mountain seems high.

220

. . . and Focus

*H*e was one of four children when his father died. His mother continued his father's old job of delivering coal, while maintaining her own job cleaning offices in downtown Pittsburgh. She was determined to keep her family together. She passed her determination on to her son, Johnny.

Johnny played football at St. Justin High School in Pittsburgh, but he didn't make the team at Notre Dame. They said he was too small, so he played for a small college team. After college he tried out for the Pittsburgh Steelers; after a short time he was cut from the team.

He then worked a construction job and played amateur football for six dollars a game. He never gave up his dream of being an NFL quarterback. Johnny wrote letters to every team in the league with a simple request: "Give me a chance—give me a try-out."

Finally the Baltimore Colts gave him that chance. He made the team and quickly became the quarterback. Within a few seasons he was arguably the best quarterback in the league. His determination led the Colts to a world championship. After setting many records he was inducted into the Football Hall of Fame. The determined quarterback's name is Johnny Unitas.

Now I can't promise you'll be a world champion, but I can promise you'll be a *life* champion if you follow the same basic principles Johnny Unitas followed.

Action Steps

1. Today I will focus my energies on specific tasks and stay with them until they are finished.
2. Today I will_____

_____

Believe in yourself, and what others think won't matter.

Ralph Waldo Emerson

. . . and Action

*T*eresa Bloomingdale says she never sees things as tragedies. In 1975, while she was seeking shelter in her basement with nine children, her house was completely blown away by a tornado. Her first thought was, "We were going to move anyway. Now I don't have to pack a thing." Now, that is an optimist! (An optimist has also been described as a man who, when his shoes are worn out, just figures that he's back on his feet.)

But that's the way Teresa Bloomingdale thinks. She decided she would like to begin writing professionally at age forty-two, when her ten children ranged in age from two to fourteen. As she recalls, "I had three preschoolers at home and two dogs. I wrote at the dining room table with the baby on my lap and a toddler playing between my legs—if he got away, he'd dismantle the house."

Teresa wrote at every opportunity. After receiving many rejection slips, she sold her first article for ten dollars. They used one paragraph from her three thousand word submission. She continued to write. She wrote her first book in 1977; in 1982 Teresa was named a contributing editor for *McCall's*. Doubleday recently signed a contract with her for two hundred and fifty thousand dollars. Teresa couldn't stop a tornado but neither could the tornado stop the optimism of Teresa Bloomingdale!

Action Steps

1. Today I will take action steps—no matter how small—that lead me toward my goal.
2. Today I will_____

Never despair; but if you do, work on in despair.

Edmund Burke

222

. . . and Vision

David W. Hartman from Philadelphia, Pennsylvania, became blind at the age of eight. He wanted to be a doctor. But when he applied to Temple University Medical School, he was told that no one without eyesight had ever completed medical school.

David decided to try it. He entered medical school at Temple and immediately faced what seemed to be an insurmountable obstacle— medical books. There were no Braille textbooks in medicine; there had never been a need for them. Furthermore, creating Braille textbooks for one student was not feasible financially. So David approached the Recording for the Blind organization, which recorded over twenty-five complete textbooks for his use. At twenty-seven, David W. Hartman received his medical degree, the first blind student to ever complete medical school.

Too often our aim is too low, our thinking too negative, our *vision* too nearsighted. What do you really want out of life? Is your goal or dream as impossible as that of an eight-year-old boy who wanted to be—and became—a doctor?

Action Steps

1. Today I will remove the limitations that my "stinkin' thinkin' " has placed on me, and will adjust my sights higher.
2. Today I will_____

_____

Until you try, you don't know what you can't do.

Henry James

. . . and Follow-through

*N*o matter what target we aim for, we seldom hit the bull's-eye on the very first try. Artillery gunners use forward observers to help them zero in on the target. Experienced archers use their first shot to judge the strength of the wind and then zero in on the following shots.

Success in business seldom if ever comes on the first effort. Athletic skills are acquired over a long period of time after hours and hours of practice. The concert pianist or violinist spends countless hours in practice and rehearsal.

As Steve Brown from Atlanta, Georgia, says, "Anything worth doing is worth doing poorly, until you learn to do it well." If we could all be skillful surgeons, scratch golfers, or Academy Award performers on our first try, then the rewards for those skills and accomplishments would be minimal at best.

It is doubtful that you will hit the target on the very first try in your attempts at success. The key is persistence and courage in the face of all those early misses. Use your first attempts to gauge exactly where you are. Learn from your mistakes and chances are good that eventually you will be hitting the bull's-eye.

Action Steps

1. Today I will return to a project I may have given up too soon, and do it poorly until I can do it well. That project is _____
_____ .

2. Today I will_____
_____

While one person hesitates because he feels inferior, the other is busy making mistakes and becoming superior.

Henry C. Link

. . . and Failure

*I*n 1958, Frank and Dan Carney operated a pizza parlor across from the family grocery store in Wichita to pay for their college education. Nineteen years later, Frank Carney sold the thirty-one-hundred outlet chain called Pizza Hut for three hundred million dollars.

Carney's advice to those starting out in business sounds strange. "You need to learn to lose." He explains it this way: "I've been involved in about fifty different business ventures and about fifteen of those worked. That means I have about a thirty percent average. But you need to be at bat and it's even more important to be at bat *after* you lose. You never learn when you are winning. You need to learn to lose."

Carney says Pizza Hut was successful because he learned from his mistakes. When an Oklahoma City expansion effort failed, he realized the importance of location and decor. When sales declined in New York, he introduced thick crusts. When regional pizza houses began to take part of the market share, he introduced Chicago-style pizza.

Carney failed many times, but he actually made his failures work for him. That's positive thinking. If you'll use your failures as stepping stones to your goals in life, I'll see you at the top!

Action Steps

1. Today I will get up to bat as often as possible and remember that I cannot hit a home run unless I take the chance of striking out.
2. Today I will_____

_____

Energy and perseverance can fit a man for almost any kind of position.
                                                      Theodore F. Merseles

... and Improvement

*I*t wasn't too many years ago that it was the kids who went to the family room to do their homework; today Mom and Dad are hitting the books, too. Ten years ago the average age of a college student was nineteen. Today it is 30, because more and more adults are enrolling in college on a full-time basis.

Marian German, a fifty-year-old grandmother, recently quit her secretarial job to work on a degree in psychology. "My children are grown," Marian says happily. "I'm free to broaden my horizons."

Maureen Promitz, a thirty-five-year-old mother, not only works full time at a medical center, she also attends night classes. She has her eye on a top level administrative spot in the medical field. Maureen says, "I want to improve, to get ahead."

Older students are more and more common in the college classroom. With our life span steadily growing longer and longer, the chances you will live into your eighties and nineties grow stronger all the time. You can make those last thirty or forty years your best years if you prepare for them. Remember, your future is exactly what you make it. Ten years from today you will be ten years older. The question to ask is will you be ten years further ahead?

Action Steps

1. Today I will begin on that worthwhile project I have been putting off.
2. Today I will_____

_____

My interest is in the future because I'm going to spend the rest of my life there.
Charles F. Kettering

. . . and Success

*J*anet Lynn was the perfect mix of grace and energy. At fifteen, she won her first of five U.S. women's figure skating titles. In 1972 she won a bronze medal at the Winter Olympics in Japan. In 1973 Janet signed a contract with the Ice Follies for $1.45 million, making her the highest-paid woman athlete in the world.

However, respiratory problems forced Janet to retire at age twenty-two. Now, twenty-nine-year-old Janet Lynn has overcome her physical ailments and is attempting a comeback. When she first resumed skating, a few minutes on the ice left her exhausted and prevented her from doing even the most simple jump. She felt like she had no muscles left. In response to the problem, Janet devised a rigorous schedule of training that helped her to improve little by little. Finally, she was able to do simple jumps; then the jumps gradually became higher, more complicated, and far more demanding.

I'm happy to tell you that Janet Lynn is back. Once again she is skating before large audiences. She has signed to skate professionally with Jo Jo Starbuck and other skating greats.

Janet Lynn had plenty of reasons to give up, but she didn't. It wasn't easy, but she will verify the oft-repeated observation that you don't pay the price *for* success, you enjoy the benefits *of* success. Let me encourage you not to give up on *your* goals in life. Janet Lynn has come a long way—and so can you.

Action Steps

1. Today I will persevere in the face of adversity.
2. Today I will_____

_____

You cannot climb the ladder of success with your hands in your pockets.

. . . and Mediocrity

A recent study shows that giving up is an acquired habit. You can learn to be persistent or determined just as easily as you can learn to give up.

Over the past few years, biologists and psychologists have been conducting experiments that confirm how powerfully our mental outlook can affect the outcome of our lives. At Johns Hopkins University, scientists have discovered that laboratory animals learn to give up. Hold a rat in your hand so firmly that no matter how hard he struggles he can't escape, and he will finally give up the struggle against the impossible odds. Then put him in a tank of water and he will not even try to swim to safety. He has learned to give up.

Although human beings are certainly not rats, we can choose our living habits. My medical friends often describe a deceased person's surrender to death in such terms as "He had nothing to live for," or "He just gave up."

Fortunately, we can make the responsible choice of optimism and hope. We can develop the habit of not giving up. We can program our minds and hearts to go on and on in the face of doubt, pain, and fear. In the process we can often conquer apparently insurmountable odds— this book is full of examples of people who have done exactly that. As a matter of fact, a major message in what I have to say is "Hang in there, and I'll see you at the top!"

Action Steps

1. Today I will begin acquiring the perseverance habit by following through on all projects to closure.
2. Today I will_____

_____

Perseverance turns the hot water of mediocrity into the steam of success.

. . . and Achievement

*H*e wrote for nine long years before a publisher accepted a book or a magazine accepted an article, but he never gave up. And that's why George Bernard Shaw became one of the world's most successful writers.

If you've read any of my previous books or heard any of my recordings, you know I'm a great believer in persistence. Whenever I speak or write I remind the audience of the tremendous importance of persistence. I'm afraid some in our society have become accustomed to instant everything. We have instant mashed potatoes, instant tea and coffee, and instant pizza, and therefore we begin to expect instant success.

But such is not the case. If you are going to be successful, you must develop persistence. How do you do that? It is not easily condensed in one simple statement, but one thing you can be sure of is that you must define your purpose. Only those who know exactly where they are going and why they want to get there can continue to get up from the failures and try again. George Bernard Shaw had definite purpose and that's why he kept plugging for nine solid years before anything was published.

Action Steps

1. Today I will identify my reasons for the things I do by asking the question "Why?"
2. Today I will_____

_____

Decide what you want, decide what you are willing to exchange for it. Establish your priorities and go to work!

H. L. Hunt

. . . and Surmounting Difficulties

*T*here are no hopeless situations, only people who lose hope in the face of situations. Kevin Poland's parents were told at his birth that he wouldn't live twenty-four hours. Later, they were told he wouldn't live past his first year. As a young boy, Kevin Poland had every reason to give up—to quit. Fortunately, those words were missing from his and his parents' vocabularies.

Kevin was in diapers until he was twelve. He has stainless steel rods in his back that enable him to sit up. Fortunately, Kevin has parents who love him enough to do what is best for him. Rather than being overprotective and fostering dependence, they have helped him by teaching independence.

As Kevin has grown up, he hasn't wanted anyone to have to care for him. He has wanted to get a job and be more self-sufficient. Kevin has been getting around in a wheelchair most of his life of seventeen years. Now he's moving on to bigger and better things. He recently passed a driver's license examination that allows him to drive his own specially equipped 1979 van. This means more freedom and more opportunity to prove wrong those who had given up on him.

It's always true that winners never quit. Kevin Poland is definitely a winner. That same spirit, dedication, and determination will also make you a winner.

Action Steps

1. Today I will think of Kevin Poland when difficult situations arise.
2. Today I will_____

> *Life affords no higher pleasure than that of surmounting difficulties, passing from one step of success to another, forming new wishes and seeing them gratified.*
>
> Dr. Samuel Johnson

. . . and Exercise

Many times people ask me how I find time to run with my travel and writing schedule. The answer is simple: I've got so much to do, I don't have time *not* to run! By running twenty-five minutes a day, five days a week, my energy level has so dramatically increased that I have at least two hours of increased productivity every day as a result of my jogging.

I'm so excited about my many involvements that I want to be able to give maximum effort for the longest period of time. Investing twenty-five minutes in running and getting two hours back is a good investment for me. There are some other benefits, too. According to a Purdue University study extending over a four-year period of time, medical bills for people who jog were substantially lower than bills for those who did not. Not only that, according to Purdue, men and women who exercised were more emotionally stable and less tense.

This really boils down to the fact that you save time and money by running or exercising. Now throw in the fact that your creativity is always higher after you exercise, and the case for physical activity is compelling—isn't it?

Action Steps

1. Today I will get involved in an exercise activity of my choice.
2. Today I will_____

_____

Exercise is to the body what prayer is to the soul.

. . . and the Musician

*M*any years ago Henry Armstrong, a young pianist and composer from Boston, set down a melody that had been running through his head for days. It was beautiful and had a lot of rhythm. For seven years he sent the song to music publishing firms in New York, but all of them turned it down. He hired a lyricist, Richard Gerard, who came up with "You're the Flower of My Heart, Sweet Rosalee," but Armstrong still could not find a publisher who was interested.

Then one day while walking down the street, Armstrong and Gerard saw a poster advertising a concert by Adelina Patti, a popular Italian singer. On impulse they decided to name their song after her. Their new title was a bit lengthy, so they reduced it to the simple phrase "Sweet Adeline." Armstrong's song became the most famous barbershop quartet ballad of all time.

The moral could simply be that a little change can make a dramatic difference, but I believe there is another real message for us. "Hang in there tough, keep thinking about your business, and keep *believing* in your dream!"

Action Steps

1. Today I will "hang in there tough" and believe in my dream.
2. Today I will_____

_____

Genius is only the power of making continuous efforts.

. . . and the Executive

*I*n none of my books, speeches, or recordings will you ever hear me tell you that life is easy, because I don't believe that it is. I think life is tough! However, I believe that if we are tough on ourselves that our life will be a great deal easier. I will tell you this—I believe life is fun, exciting, and rewarding!

A study by the Institute of Investor Opinion made for C. Stewart Baeder Associates, a New York City executive search firm, reveals something rather intriguing that supports these statements. The survey shows that of the chief executive officers of one hundred and fifty major U.S. companies, more than two out of three included self-discipline in profiles of the type of successor they would recommend. Eighty-nine percent rated self-discipline as very important. As a matter of fact, the ability and willingness to discipline oneself to "hang in there" was the most important and highest-rated qualification they were looking for.

I believe firmly that if we're tough on ourselves, life will be easier on us. Follow this maxim and the doors of opportunity will spring open wider and more often for you.

Action Steps

1. Today I will rate self-discipline as the most important qualification that I am looking for.
2. Today I will_____

_____

He who reigns within himself, and rules passions, desires, and fears, is more than a king.

. . . and Half-Hearted Effort

*W*hen I was a boy my friends and I often spent hot summer days diving out of a sycamore tree at a nearby creek. A couple of my buddies learned some fancy dives that just about anyone would have been proud to emulate. They could turn a complete forward flip and hit the water with precision. On these dives, it was all or nothing. There could be no half-hearted commitment, because the slightest hesitation usually produced a stinging belly-buster.

This principle is true in almost every area of life. It is impossible to succeed if our commitment is only half-hearted, for when things get tough and we need that extra effort, it will not be there. When you only dabble in, do just a bit of, or take a shot at something, or just give it a whirl, the result is inevitably a painful belly-buster.

In the success and happiness game, it's all or nothing. Total commitment is a key to your success, so give it your very best. The difference between success and failure is often the difference between a half-hearted effort and total commitment!

Action Steps

1. Today I will recognize that commitment is the primary key to achieving my goals.
2. Today I will_____

_____

You cannot escape the responsibility of tomorrow by evading it today.
                                                          Abraham Lincoln

. . . and the Little Things

*D*uring an interview several years after his retirement, Ty Cobb was asked why he was so nervous every time he got on first base. The great baseball player for Detroit indignantly replied that he was not nervous. The reporter, wishing to make light of his observation, jokingly said, "Now, Mr. Cobb, every time I saw you on first base you would continuously kick the bag until the pitcher was ready to pitch. Now, if that's not being nervous, what is it?"

Ty Cobb looked at him, smiled, and said, "Son, let me explain something to you. I was *definitely* not nervous while I was on first base. But very early in my career, I discovered that if I kicked the first base bag enough times, that I could move it a full two inches towards second base, which gave me that much of a jump towards stealing that base!"

Is it any wonder that Ty Cobb held the record for the most stolen bases for nearly half a century, until Lou Brock came along and broke that record? Yes, it's the little things that make the big difference in baseball, as well as in life.

Action Steps

1. Today I will do whatever possible to take advantage of any and all opportunities that are presented to me.
2. Today I will_____

_____

Luck is the sense to recognize an opportunity and the ability to take advantage of it.

. . . and Retirement

*H*alf the workers reaching the age of sixty-five stay on the job, according to a study of several major industries. The reasons are many and varied, but one possibility is that managers are realizing the value of experience and wisdom in the company. According to Edwin Miller's book, *Management of Human Resources,* creative activity is lowest in the twenty-one-to-fifty-year-old age group. In the group over the age of fifty, this creative activity begins to increase—not to decrease, as some might think.

In sales personnel, for example, the peak performance of a clerk is not reached until the age of fifty-five. Older clerks are generally the most dependable and competent because of years of experience in working with people. Managers need to be aware of the value of older workers. If you are in the fifty-and-over bracket, you too must realize that your most creative years are ahead of you.

Even if you are forced into retirement from one career, you have much wisdom and experience that is needed in the marketplace. Hang in there folks, the best is yet to come!

Action Steps

1. Today I will remember that despite my age, the best is yet to come!
2. Today I will_____

_____

Age should not have its face lifted, but it should rather teach the world to admire wrinkles as the etchings of experience and the firm lines of character.
                                                            Ralph Barton Perry

. . . The Winner's Edge

*T*he *Winner's Edge* sounds like a good book title, which is exactly what it is. Bob Oates, Jr., has compiled some comments and reflections on the mysterious difference between winning and losing.

O. J. Simpson says, "It requires character to be a winner, and character is simply self-knowledge." Dan Dierdorf, the all-pro tackle, agrees. "I must know me first. I don't worry about the other guy, because if my technique is right I know I can't be beaten."

Good attitude for any business, wouldn't you say? Roger Staubach believes the edge is confidence born of preparation. "Confidence in the last two minutes of a playoff game comes from days, weeks, months, and even years of very hard work."

Interesting, isn't it, how each of those winning principles can be so easily applied to our own business and personal lives? I'm betting that you will be able to apply these principles to your life. Then you, too, will have the winner's edge and will be an even bigger winner!

Action Steps

1. Today I will get to know me first, and concentrate on my technique, knowing full well that if I take care of myself that I can't be beaten.
2. Today I will_____

_____

The measure of a man's real character is what he would do if he knew he would never be found out.

. . . and the Target

*P*ersistence is a key ingredient in the success of any endeavor, whether it be selling, football, or even the development of a happy marriage. The salesman must persist in his selling technique, and the successful football team will consistently pound away at the weakness of the opponent's defense.

If you are now working on a project that seems to be bogged down or stalled at a certain level, let me urge you to follow the advice of the writer Stendahl. "If you are going to reach your goal, you must continue to fire on the target."

Narrow your objective, be specific about your target, get it down to details, and keep firing. Your best chance for victory lies in the relentless pursuit of your goal. Aim at the bull's-eye and continue to fire. Even when things seem to be at a standstill or when the obstacles seem insurmountable, you must have the courage and the confidence to keep plugging away.

Action Steps

1. Today I will identify my target and continue to fire on that target.
2. Today I will_____

_____

Failure is often the line of least persistence.

. . . and Selling

All of us are salespeople. Some of us are salespeople in the strict sense of the word—we sell products, and that means we make calls. But actually, we are all salespeople. You may not sell a particular product, but you are constantly trying to sell your ideas or opinions.

Did you know that for regular salespeople, most of the sales come on the first or second call to a particular customer? Only seven percent come on a third call. The obvious conclusion is not to spend too much time on those third calls. Concentrate on the first and second efforts!

When you are trying to sell yourself to an employer there are three things to remember. (These principles will also work if you are trying to sell an idea to your boss, or anything at all to anyone.) First, be prepared. Learn as much about your prospective employer and his business as you can. Second, ask some questions. Get the prospective employer talking and you will be able to discover what he is most interested in and how you can best be of service. Third, make your points with enthusiasm.

Take a look at the last four letters in the word *enthusiasm*. These letters form an acrostic that stands for the phrase "I am sold myself." Now, if you really are sold that you can do a job and be a valuable employee, I'll just bet that you can sell that prospective employer on giving you a chance to do exactly that!

Action Steps

1. Today I will remember that if "I am sold myself," I will be enthusiastic. This will help me to sell to whomever I am trying to sell.
2. Today I will_____

The worst bankruptcy in the world is the man who has lost his enthusiasm. Let a man lose everything else in the world but his enthusiasm and he will come through again to success.

H. W. Arnold

239